SELECTED POEMS AND LETTERS

J. R.
to G. B.
1917.

Isaac Rosenberg

Selected Poems and Letters

Edited and introduced
by
Jean Liddiard

ENITHARMON PRESS
in association with

THE EUROPEAN JEWISH PUBLICATIONS SOCIETY

First published in 2003
by the Enitharmon Press
26B Caversham Road
London NW5 2DU
www.enitharmon.co.uk

in association with The European Jewish Publications Society,
PO Box 19948, London N3 3ZJ.
website: www.ejps.org.uk

*The European Jewish Publications Society is a registered charity which
gives grants to assist in the publication and distribution of books relevant
to Jewish literature, history, religion, philosophy, politics and culture.*

Distributed in the UK by
Central Books
99 Wallis Road
London E9 5LN

Distributed in the USA and Canada
by Dufour Editions Inc.
PO Box 7, Chester Springs
PA 19425, USA

ISBN 1 900564 89 0

Enitharmon Press gratefully acknowledges the financial support of
Arts Council England, London.

British Library Cataloguing-in-Publication Data.
A catalogue record for this book is available
from the British Library.

The frontispiece shows a photograph of Isaac Rosenberg
in the uniform of the King's Own Royal Lancasters,
inscribed in his hand 'IR to GB 1917'; sent by Rosenberg
to Gordon Bottomley.

Typeset in Caslon by Servis Filmsetting Ltd
and printed in England by
The Cromwell Press.

For Isaac Horvitch
and the Rosenberg family descendants,
with grateful thanks for their support and generosity
on behalf of Isaac Rosenberg

Self Portrait in a Pink Tie (1914, Imperial War Museum)

CONTENTS

7

CHRONOLOGICAL SUMMARY OF THE LIFE OF ISAAC ROSENBERG

1890 25 November. Isaac Rosenberg born at 5 Adelaide Place Bristol, eldest son and second child of Barnett (or Barnard) and Anna Rosenberg. Their first child, a daughter Minnie, had been born in Lithuania in 1887. In 1887 or 1888 Barnett had emigrated to England from Lithuania, followed by his wife and child. From Leeds in Yorkshire they moved to Bristol.

1892 Sister Annie born in Bristol.

1894 Sister Rachel born in Bristol.

1897 Brother David born in Bristol. Family moves to 47 Cable Street, Stepney, London East. Isaac enrols at St Paul's School, Wellclose Square, St George's in the East.

1899 Brother Elkon born.

14 November. Isaac enrols at Baker Street School, Stepney East.

1900? Family move to 58 Jubilee Street, Stepney, becoming neighbours of J. H. Amschewitz, a professional artist who encourages Isaac and introduces him to the schoolteacher Winifreda Seaton. She befriends and corresponds with him until his death.

1902 Isaac begins special classes at Stepney Green Art School, sent by his headmaster.

1905   Isaac is apprenticed to Carl Hentschel's, Engravers of Fleet Street.

1907   Family moves to 159 Oxford Street, London East. Isaac starts evening classes at London School of Photo-engraving and Lithography, Bolt Court, Fleet Street. At Amschewitz's suggestion Isaac attends evening classes at Birkbeck College and is taught by Alice Wright who discusses poetry with him and corresponds with him until his death.

1911   Isaac meets young Jewish writers and artists Samuel Winsten, Joseph Leftwich and John Rodker, who form a group centred on the Whitechapel Library and Art Gallery in East London.

17 March. Isaac meets Lily Delissa Joseph (sister of the artist Solomon J. Solomon RA); taken on as her son's art tutor, he meets her sister Mrs Henrietta Löwy, and Mrs Herbert Cohen.

13 October. Isaac joins the Slade School of Fine Art, sponsored by the above ladies. Mrs Löwy's daughter Ruth is a fellow student. (She later marries the publisher Victor Gollancz.)

1912   Isaac writes to and meets Laurence Binyon, poet and Keeper of Prints and Drawings at the British Museum, who corresponds with him and writes Introductory Memoir to 1922 edition of Isaac's selected poems.

Spring/summer. Isaac produces 50 copies of his first 24-page pamphlet of poems *Night and Day*, printed for him by Israel Narodiczky for £2.

Winter. Rosenberg family moves to 87 Dempsey Street, Stepney East.

Isaac has disagreements with his patrons and instead receives funds from Jewish Educational Aid Society until he leaves the Slade in 1914.

1913   Summer. Isaac spends holiday to recover failing health in Sandown, Isle of Wight, accompanied by Whitechapel friend and fellow Slade student, the artist David Bomberg.

November. The artist Mark Gertler, another Whitechapel companion and fellow Slade student, introduces Isaac at the Café Royal to the poet T. E. Hulme and to Edward Marsh, private secretary to Winston Churchill and a patron of the arts, who published five volumes of the popular anthology *Georgian Poetry*. Marsh buys Isaac's pictures, writes regularly to him and encourages his poetry.

1914   March. Isaac leaves Slade School of Fine Art.

May. Isaac exhibits at Whitechapel Art Gallery's Exhibition of Twentieth Century Artists.

June. Isaac, unable to find work and in poor health, sails for South Africa to stay with his sister Minnie, who had moved to Cape Town in 1913 with her husband Wolf Horvitch.

July. Completes some paintings and gives lectures on art, published with two poems in magazine *South African Women in Council*.

1914   4 August. Great Britain declares war on Germany.

1915   March. Isaac arrives back home in Dempsey Street.

April. Isaac produces 100 copies of his second pamphlet of poems, *Youth*, printed by Israel Narodiczky for £2.10s, paid for by selling three pictures to Edward Marsh.

May. Isaac meets the author Sydney Schiff (pen name Stephen Hudson) at the Café Royal. He read Isaac's poems and corresponded with him until his death.

June/July/August. *Colour* magazine edited by T. M. Wood prints 'Heart's First Word', 'A Girl's Thoughts' and 'Wedded' (1).

September. Isaac starts evening classes in block-making, but fails to find work.

October. Isaac enlists and is sent to Recruiting Depot at Bury St Edmunds, Suffolk, to join Bantam Battalion of 12 Suffolk Regiment 40th Division, as he is too short for other units.

November. In hospital with cut hands after a fall. Lascelles Abercrombie (1881–1931), poet, critic, later professor at Leeds and London universities, starts correspondence with Isaac after his friend Marsh shows him Isaac's poems.

1916   16 January. After four days' Christmas home leave Isaac transferred to 12th South Lancashires, Blackdown Camp, Farnborough, Hants.

March. Isaac transferred again to 11th Battalion King's Own Royal Lancasters at Blackdown Camp as Private Isaac Rosenberg, no. 22311.

19 May. During six days' embarkation leave Reuben Cohen of Narodiczky's (under name of Paragon Printing Works) prints Isaac's last pamphlet *Moses*.

(?)2 June. Isaac embarks with his unit for France.

June. In mid-June Isaac begins a correspondence lasting until his death with two older poets, R. C. Trevelyan

(1872–1951), poet and translator from classical literature, and Gordon Bottomley (1874–1948), Georgian poet and dramatist. Bottomley encouraged Isaac in life and preserved his reputation and many of his manuscripts after his death, editing and selecting the *Poems by Isaac Rosenberg* (Heinemann, 1922), and co-editing with D. W. Harding the *Collected Works* (Chatto and Windus,1937).

August. Isaac's unit moves into trenches.

September. Isaac sends 'Break of Day in the Trenches' to Harriet Monroe of *Poetry* (Chicago).

25 November. Isaac's 26th birthday.

December. Harriet Monroe prints 'Marching' (sent in by John Rodker in January 1916) and 'Break of Day in the Trenches' in *Poetry* (Chicago).

1917   January. Isaac's health fails and he is assigned to a Works Battalion behind the lines.

Early May. Isaac's health improves and in a letter to Marsh he mentions 'Dead Man's Dump'.

Late May. Isaac writes to Marsh again about 'Dead Man's Dump' and another poem, almost certainly 'Daughters of War', as well mentioning his play *The Amulet*.

June. Isaac reassigned to 229 Field Company Royal Engineers, attached to 11th Battalion K.O.R.L.

July/August. Isaac writes to Marsh and Bottomley about the drafts of his play, now called *The Unicorn*.

16 September. Isaac at home on leave for ten days; in contact with Bottomley, Schiff and Trevelyan. Meets scholar and critic Jacob ('Jack') Isaacs at Café Royal.

13

Late September. *Georgian Poetry* (edited by Marsh) published, including extract 'Ah! Koelue!' from Isaac's play *Moses*.

Late October. Isaac admitted to 51st General Hospital with influenza and remains there until December. In a letter to his boyhood friend Leftwich, refers to his two soldier brothers also being in hospital.

1918 Late January. Isaac back in the trenches with 4th Platoon A Company 11th K.O.R.L..

7 February. Isaac transferred to 8th Platoon B Company 1st Battalion K.O.R.L.in the 4th Division, after 11th Battalion broke up owing to shortage of men.

Early March. Isaac writes to Marsh that he has requested a transfer to the Jewish Battalion in Mesopotamia. Isaac manages to meet his brother David.

11 March. Isaac's 1st K.O.R.L. Battalion moves to Arras for training.

19 March. Isaac's battalion moves into front line, the Greenland Hill Sector near Arras, until 24 March.

28 March. 1st Battalion K.O.R.L moves back into front line. Isaac writes his last letter to March enclosing his final poem, 'Through these pale cold days'. The Germans launch full-scale attack and Isaac's battalion loses seventy men.

31 March. Isaac detailed for a wiring patrol that night.

1 April. Isaac fails to return. His remains are later found with those of his comrades.

Private Isaac Rosenberg no. 22311 is buried in Bailleul Road East British Cemetery, north-east of Arras in Northern France.

PUBLICATIONS AND COLLECTIONS OF MANUSCRIPTS, PAINTINGS AND DRAWINGS

Isaac Rosenberg published very little in his lifetime and his *Collected Works* (Chatto and Windus, 1937) went out of print soon afterwards, until his publisher Ian Parsons, joint literary executor with the poet Patric Dickinson, brought out a new edition in 1979. This too has long been out of print. Now a complete and revised variorum edition of the poems and plays, newly edited by Dr Vivien Noakes, is in preparation with Oxford University Press.

The text for this present edition of *Selected Poems and Letters* is based on the 1979 Chatto and Windus *Collected Works*. In his Editor's Note Ian Parsons set out his editorial principles as follows: 'I have endeavoured to stick as closely as possible to the texts of the poems as he left them, only departing from them when there was some compelling reason for doing so, and always indicating the fact by square brackets or a footnote. With the Letters, on the other hand, I have thought it right to make them as easy as possible to read and understand. This has involved a certain (though very limited) amount of 'editing' in the matter of punctuation, spelling, and the occasional grammatical solecism.'

Publications during Rosenberg's lifetime

Night and Day: pamphlet of poems, 24pp, 50 copies printed for Rosenberg by Israel Narodiczky for £2 (1912).

Youth: pamphlet of poems, 100 copies printed for Rosenberg by Israel Narodiczky for £2. 10sh. (April 1915).

Colour: magazine edited by T. M. Wood, publishes 'Heart's First Word' (June), 'A Girl's Thoughts '(July) and 'Wedded' (1) (August) 1915.

Moses: pamphlet of poems and verse play, printed for Rosenberg by Reuben Cohen of Narodiczky's under name of 'Paragon Printing Works 8 Ocean Street Stepney Green'. Rosenberg offered them for sale to friends at 1s or cloth bound 4/6d each, May 1916.

Poetry (Chicago) magazine, edited by Harriet Monroe, published 'Marching' and 'Break of Day in the Trenches', December 1916.

Georgian Poetry 1916–17 volume 3, anthology compiled by Edward Marsh, published by Harold Monro of The Poetry Bookshop, included 'Ah! Koelue!', extract from Rosenberg's play *Moses* (September 1917).

Publications after Rosenberg's death

Poems by Isaac Rosenberg, selected and edited by Gordon Bottomley, with an Introductory Memoir by Laurence Binyon, London: William Heinemann, 1922.

The Collected Works of Isaac Rosenberg, edited by Gordon Bottomley and Denys Harding, with a Foreword by Siegfried Sassoon, London: Chatto and Windus, 1937.

Poems by Isaac Rosenberg, Compact Poets paperback, selected and introduced by Denys Harding, London: Chatto and Windus, 1972.

The Collected Works of Isaac Rosenberg, Poetry, Prose, Letters, Paintings and Drawings with a Foreword by Siegfried Sassoon, edited with Introduction and Notes by Ian Parsons, London: Chatto and Windus, 1979.

Collections of Manuscripts, Paintings and Drawings

The British Library, London, holds a collection of poems and letters.
The British Museum Prints and Drawings Department, London holds a collection of drawings.

The Imperial War Museum, London, holds a collection of manuscript poems, letters, paintings and photographs.
The Berg Collection at the New York Public Library holds Edward Marsh's collection of correspondence, including Rosenberg's letters to him.
The Slade School of Fine Art, London, holds some paintings.
Tate Britain and the National Portrait Gallery in London each hold a self-portrait.

Further Reading

Isaac Rosenberg: The Half Used Life, by Jean Liddiard, London: Victor Gollancz, 1975.

Isaac Rosenberg 1890–1918: A Poet and Painter of the First World War, catalogue for National Book League Exhibition Word and Image VI, by Jean Liddiard, London: National Book League, 1975.

Journey to the Trenches: the Life of Isaac Rosenberg 1890–1918, by Joseph Cohen, London: Robson Books, 1975.

Isaac Rosenberg: Poet and Painter, by Jean Moorcroft Wilson, London: Cecil Woolf, 1975.

INTRODUCTION

Isaac Rosenberg, a major poet of the First World War and a talented painter, was born on 25 November 1890, to Jewish immigrant parents from Lithuania living in Bristol. While still a young child he moved with his family to Stepney in the East End of London. Obliged to leave school at fourteen and earn his living as an apprentice engraver, he snatched what time he could for drawing and writing. In the evenings after work he frequented the Whitechapel Library and Art Gallery in the East End with his friends, the painters Mark Gertler and David Bomberg, and the poet John Rodker. Here they benefited from the help of its remarkable librarian, Morley Dainow. Afterwards they would walk the streets discussing art and poetry, pausing under lamp-posts to read each other's poems. One of these companions was Joseph Leftwich, later a leading member of the Anglo-Jewish cultural community, who in his own book of poems of 1937 recalled the impact Rosenberg made on their group: 'I began to write verse in 1911, under the influence of my friend Isaac Rosenberg. Not that he told me what to write or bothered much about what I wrote. He was too self-absorbed to do that ...My other friend of that period, John Rodker, had also been writing before we met Rosenberg in 1911...Rosenberg had been writing poetry for years, and we three immediately recognised his extraordinary ability.'

In 1911 Rosenberg was noticed copying paintings at the National Gallery by some wealthy Jewish ladies who later clubbed together to send him to the Slade School of Fine Art, where most of the interesting painters of the time were trained. As well as his East End friends Mark Gertler and David Bomberg, there were students such as Stanley and Gilbert Spencer, Dora Carrington and Christopher Wynne Nevinson. All these became well-known artists of the period before and during the First World War. The Slade students were excited by the Modernist, Post-Impressionist and Cubist ideas flowing across the Channel and Rosenberg reflected these when he wrote about what he was learning at the Slade: 'a sharp contour means more than the blending of tone into tone…the concise pregnant quality of poetry rather than prose.'

His most memorable images are his series of self-portraits. One is held by Tate Britain, another by the National Portrait Gallery, and others, with most of his remaining paintings, by the Imperial War Museum, while Rosenberg's family retain some pictures and drawings. Many of his manuscripts and drawings may also be found at the British Library and the Imperial War Museum.

Passionate in his pursuit of art and poetry, he persisted in seeking out not only his like-minded contemporaries but also others, usually older, who could help him as mentors and patrons, through encouragement, professional expertise or practical support. It is characteristic of Rosenberg's strength of personality that all those he encountered remembered him for years afterwards, while many continued to correspond with him until his death in 1918. Through a neighbour, the professional artist J. H. Amschewitz, he met Alice Wright, a tutor at Birkbeck College who taught him at evening art classes, introducing him to the work of William Blake. It was also through Amschewitz that he met Winifreda Seaton, a middle-aged schoolteacher who lent him books on the Metaphysical poets. From his response, revealing his great thirst for poetry, it is clear why for all his sometimes awkward and prickly temperament, his correspondents found him so rewarding: 'Poetical appreciation is only newly bursting on me. I always enjoyed Shelley and Keats. The "Hyperion" ravished me…'.

The confidence Rosenberg lacked in his personal relationships did not extend to his artistic ones. Where his poetry and painting were concerned he was not afraid to bring himself to the notice of those who could advise and assist him. The first established poet whom Rosenberg encountered was Laurence Binyon, Keeper of Prints and Drawings at the British Museum. Characteristically, it was Rosenberg who approached Binyon to introduce himself, as Binyon remembered in his 1922 selection of the *Poems of Isaac Rosenberg*:

I cannot fix precisely the date, but it must have been some time in 1912, when one morning there came to me a letter in an untidy hand from an address in Whitechapel, enclosing some pages of verse on which criticism was asked, and signed 'Isaac Rosenberg'. It was impossible not to be struck by something unusual in the quality of the poems…At my invitation Rosenberg came to see me. Small in stature, dark, bright-eyed, thoroughly Jewish in type, he seemed a boy with an unusual mixture of self-reliance and modesty. Indeed, no-one could have had a more independent nature. Obviously sensitive, he was not touchy or aggressive. Possessed of vivid enthusiasms, he was shy in speech. One found in talk how strangely little of second-hand (in one of his age) there was in his opinions, how fresh a mind he brought to what he saw and read. There was an odd kind of charm in his manner which came from his earnest, transparent sincerity.

At the Café Royal in November 1913, Mark Gertler introduced Rosenberg to the Imagist poet T. E. Hulme and to Edward Marsh, a senior civil servant who was private secretary to Winston Churchill, yet whose private life and small private income was devoted to the support of artists and writers. He bought their paintings and drawings and under the influence of the young Cambridge poet Rupert Brooke initiated publication of five volumes of contemporary poetry between 1912 and 1922, with the title *Georgian Poetry*. Marsh became Rosenberg's most important patron, buying his drawings and paintings, including his major picture *Sacred Love*, and publishing a lyric extract from his verse play *Moses* in *Georgian Poetry 1916–17*. Through him Rosenberg later corresponded with two more supporters, the older Georgian poets Gordon Bottomley and Lascelles Abercrombie.

Later readers of Rosenberg, including his editor and publisher Ian Parsons, while acknowledging the invaluable moral and practical support this Georgian group gave him, have deplored its influence on his poetry, and wished that Rosenberg could have benefited from a more up-to-date mentor, rather as Wilfred Owen did from Siegfried Sassoon. Rosenberg never met Sassoon, but Sassoon wrote the foreword to the first posthumous *Collected Works* in 1937. Sassoon saw 'a fruitful fusion between English and Hebrew culture...His experiments were a strenuous effort for impassioned expression; his imagination had a sinewy and muscular aliveness...he *modelled* words with fierce energy and aspiration, finding ecstasy in form, dreaming in grandeurs of superb light and deep shadow; his poetic visions are mostly in sombre colours and looming sculptural masses, molten and amply wrought.' Here Sassoon has perceived how the eye and imagination of both painter and poet come together to give Rosenberg's work its particular sensuous vividness and visionary reach.

At the Café Royal, however, Rosenberg did meet two poets whose work was very different from the rather English middle-class preoccupations of the 'Georgian' poets. W. B. Yeats, whom he called 'the established great man', shared with Rosenberg the position of outsider, being *in* but not *of* English culture. Neither had experienced the traditional classical university education, and as Yeats was to develop his own poetic world through the story of Ireland, so Rosenberg was to create his own vision, unhampered but perhaps modified by his own East End Jewish background, when confronted by a situation without precedent on the Western Front. Yeats drew Rosenberg to the attention of Ezra Pound, who was deeply involved with the making of a new poetry for a new century, and who, in the words of poet Richard Aldington, was 'great fun, a small but persistent volcano in the dim levels of London literary society'. Pound's panache probably inhibited Rosenberg, yet he recommended Rosenberg's pamphlet *Youth* to his friend Harriet Monroe, publisher of the important literary magazine *Poetry* (Chicago), and she eventually printed 'Break of Day in the Trenches' and 'Marching' in December 1916. But the differences in background and temperament were too wide, and while Rosenberg's seriousness and tenacity clearly impressed both Yeats and Pound, his personality, at once diffident and single minded, was not an easy one in a difficult social situation with poets already confident of recognition and attention. Yeats and Pound were as self-absorbed in their own way as Rosenberg, and the fuller attention and sympathy he received from his older and perhaps less glamorous poet correspondents gave him the sustained emotional and intellectual support he desperately needed in his isolation, especially in the trenches. Unlike Yeats and Pound, Robert Graves served on the Western Front. In his *Contemporary Techniques of Poetry* (1925) he likened the state of English poetry to politics, placing the traditional established poets (like the former Poet Laureate Alfred Austin) on the right, the Georgians (like Binyon, Abercrombie and Bottomley, who roughly speaking made leftward excursions from a traditional base) in the centre, and the avant-garde (Pound, the Imagists, Futurists and so on) on the left. Graves, who never met Rosenberg, nonetheless singled him out for individual comment: 'there are, besides, born revolutionaries like Isaac Rosenberg'.

As Graves noticed, Rosenberg against the odds was trying to do something radical, and was not about to be aligned with a particular group, whether traditional or avant-garde. At a time when the forces of Modernism were fracturing the cultural landscape and groups were forming and reforming to attract attention and publication, to stand alone was a brave venture for any poet, let alone for one as isolated as Rosenberg. In his work, as in his life, he never lacked courage and endurance; he never gave up or settled for less, and while his ambition sometimes resulted in failure, when he succeeded he achieved some of the greatest poems of his time. He tried to explain this necessary risk-taking to Winifreda Seaton in 1917:

> Everyone has agreed with you about the faults, and the reason is obvious; the faults are so glaring that nobody can fail to see them. But how many have seen the beauties? And it is here more than the other that the true critic shows himself. And I absolutely disagree that it is blindness or carelessness; it is the brain succumbing to the herculean attempt to enrich the world of ideas.

After leaving the Slade in March 1914 he found himself once again out of work, short of money and with a persistent cough. The only positive development was an exhibition at the Whitechapel Gallery in May and June, organised by his old friend and fellow Slade student David Bomberg. Already one of the acknowledged leaders of the avant-garde in painting by virtue of his Cubist experiments, Bomberg included work by all his Slade contemporaries, including five works by Rosenberg. In a lecture on modern art he was to give in South Africa later that year, Rosenberg described the ferment Modernism was stirring up in the art world:

> Art is now, as it were, a volcano. Eruptions are continual, and immense cities of culture at its foot are shaken and shivered. The roots of a dead universe are torn up by hands, feverish and consuming with an exuberant vitality – and amid dynamic threatenings we watch the hastening of the corroding doom.

In his painting, as in his poetry, Rosenberg would maintain his own vision. As with his poetry, he did not succumb to the lure of the group movement. Alert to the impact of the Post-Impressionists who had been famously first exhibited by the critic Roger Fry in London in 1910, he responded also to the vitality of his friend Bomberg's Cubism, while refusing himself to become a partisan: 'the symbols they use are symbols of symbols. But they have introduced urgency-energy into art and striven to connect it more with life.'

Here is a clue to the self-sufficiency and the persistence of this taciturn young man in pursuing his own artistic route; while acknowledging his thirst for contact with other poets, artists and men of letters such as Marsh, he had already learnt to hold his own with the talented, opinionated and argumentative friends of his youth such as Bomberg and Rodker. As the acknowledged poet of that lively group he was not to be thrown even by the formidable literary scene of the Café Royal, its bohemian Domino Room the famous haunt of writers and artists since the days of Oscar Wilde.

Urged by his anxious family, Rosenberg applied for a grant from the Jewish Educational Aid Society which enabled him to visit his married sister Minnie in South Africa to improve his health and earn some money through painting. It was the last time in his life that he was free to devote himself to his art: 'There's a lot of splendid stuff to paint. We are walled in by the sharp upright mountain and the bay. Across the bay the piled-up mountains of Africa look lovely and dangerous. It makes one think of savagery and earthquakes – the elemental lawlessness.'

Much of what he produced while he was there has disappeared.

There is an unconfirmed anecdote that he lost some pictures overboard on the voyage home, but some self-portraits have survived, including the one reproduced on the cover of this book. While Rosenberg was in South Africa, war was declared. In contrast to the outpouring of patriotic fervour which had affected the poets back home, Rosenberg's first response to the war was distanced, cool and ominous:

> Snow is a strange white word;
> No ice or frost
> Has asked of bud or bird
> For Winter's cost.

In spite of family pressure to stay, he felt restless and cut off in South Africa, and came home in the spring of 1915. By April of that year the British regular army had been effectively destroyed at the battles of Neuve-Chapelle and Ypres, and Lord Kitchener's famous recruiting poster with the pointing finger had appeared demanding more volunteers. The change to Britain now on a war footing must have been very marked to the newly returned traveller. The old Café Royal crowd was depleted and scattered, its habitués such as T. E. Hulme and the artists C. W. R. Nevinson and Gaudier-Brzeska either on their way to war or busy with the war effort. Edward Marsh was at the Admiralty with Winston Churchill, preparing for an expedition to the Dardanelles to attack German's ally Turkey. It was on the way to this invasion that Marsh's friend Rupert Brooke died. Dean Inge had earlier quoted his poem 'The Soldier' in St Paul's Cathedral and when, after his death, Churchill (who had met Brooke through Marsh) spoke of 'the poet-soldier' in a letter to *The Times*, Brooke became a symbol overnight. Rosenberg had not cared for what he called Brooke's 'begloried sonnets', and in a characteristically direct letter to Mrs Cohen he marks out quite clearly the difference in his own approach to Brooke's: 'what I mean is second hand phrases "lambent fires" &c takes from the reality and strength. It should be approached in a colder way, with less of the million feelings everybody feels.'

However, it was Brooke's poetry that had restored the glamour to an increasingly brutal and bewildering war and had caught the national mood. Meanwhile Rosenberg was printing at his own expense his pamphlet of poems *Youth*, which is clearly about growing up. He grouped his poems in three parts: 'Faith and Fear', 'The Cynic's Lamp' and 'Sunfire'. He was as usual looking for work and short of money. He was later to write to a new mentor, the novelist Sydney Schiff, in September 1915: 'forgive this private cry but even the enormity of what is going on all through Europe always seems less to an individual than his own private struggle.'

Pressures were mounting on any young man who was not in khaki, and Rosenberg's Whitechapel group were all affected by it. Their Jewish upbringing had imbued them all with a passionate belief in the evils of war. Rosenberg told another poet correspondent in 1916: 'my people are all Tolstoylians and object to my being in khaki' (*sic*). But private convictions were no longer enough. Without work Rosenberg felt helpless and cut off from meaningful activity – perhaps expressed at this time in his poem 'Chagrin':

> Christ! end this hanging death,
> For endlessness hangs therefrom.

In June 1915 he wrote to Schiff: 'I am thinking of enlisting if they will have me, though it is against all my principles of justice – though I would be doing the most criminal thing a man can do – I am so sure my mother would not stand the shock that I don't know what to do.'

Five of Rosenberg's friends became conscientious objectors, including John Rodker and Mark Gertler, and some like Rodker and Samuel Winsten were imprisoned for their beliefs. Rosenberg as usual was not one for parading his private feelings. But he must have discussed them with Rodker and Gertler during that summer. His dilemma emerged again in a letter to Schiff that autumn: 'I have changed my mind again about joining the army. I feel about it that more men means more war, – beside the immorality of joining without patriotic convictions.'

26

Rosenberg did not feel the emotional commitment to an ideal pastoral England expressed in the poetry of Georgians like Rupert Brooke. As a Jew brought up in the East End of London his experience of English culture was naturally very different. His allegiances were to English poets rather than to a tradition of English poetry, and to friends and family rather than to an abstract conception of 'England'. Equally his pacifist background made him react as strongly as his other contemporaries to German militarism, as in his poem on the sinking of the liner *Lusitania* on 7 May 1915:

> Now you have got the peace-faring *Lusitania*,
> Germany's gift – all earth they would give thee, Chaos.

Then, in October 1915, Rosenberg suddenly disappeared. Without telling even his family, he had enlisted as a private soldier at a recruiting station in Whitehall. Schiff received a letter from Bury St Edmunds:

> I could not get the work I thought I might so I have joined this Bantam Battalion (as I was too short for any other) which seems to be the most rascally affair in the world. I have to eat out of a basin together with some horribly smelling scavenger who spits and sneezes into it etc…Besides my being a Jew makes it bad amongst these wretches.

Rosenberg was caught up in the confusion of an army overwhelmed by unprecedented numbers of volunteers. While still with the Suffolks in December 1915, he wrote to Marsh for help with sorting out payment to his mother:

> I never joined the army from patriotic reasons. Nothing can justify war. I suppose we must all fight to get the trouble over… I thought if I'd join there would be the separation allowance for my mother. At Whitehall it was fixed up that 16/6 would be given including the 3/6 a week deducted from my 7/–. Its now between 2 and 3 months since I joined; my 3/6 is deducted right enough, but my mother hasn't received a farthing…[*sic*]

27

In the late spring of 1916 before his battalion was sent overseas he came home for a few days' leave to visit his mother, and saw through the press his final pamphlet of poems, *Moses*, which included his play of that name. His unfit Bantam Battalion was broken up, and because of the manpower shortage in the northern regiments (caused by the need for reserved industrial occupations) he eventually ended up in the regiment of the King's Own Royal Lancasters, as Private 22311, A Company, 11th Battalion. On 2 June 1916 they embarked for France. During the voyage he wrote 'The Troop Ship' and, as he began doing from then onwards, he sent the poem straight home to his sister Annie for typing out and safe-keeping. On 1 July 1916 the British Army began the Somme Offensive, sustaining 60,000 casualties on that day alone. Rosenberg's division, the 40th, was inexorably drawn southward to replace those divisions sucked into the Somme battle. In August he sent home 'August 1914':

> Three lives hath one life –
> Iron, honey, gold.
> The gold, the honey gone –
> Left is the hard and cold.

As a private soldier Rosenberg had no privacy, nowhere to keep personal possessions such as books – except his pack, and certainly nowhere warm, dry and well-lit to read or write. His letters are full of thanks for small gifts that kept him going: pencil and paper, cigarettes, boxes of chocolates and small sums of money. Behind the lines he used YMCA notepaper to set down his verses, and had to find a bit of candle or campfire for light. He explained to Marsh in May 1917, that 'It is only when we get a bit of rest and the others might be gambling or squabbling I add a line or two, and continue this way'.

It was astonishing that as a private soldier in the trenches he managed to write anything at all, yet he sent home, scribbled in pencil on scraps of paper, poems that were among the greatest produced during the war. He retained the tenacity amongst the routine physical privations of the trenches to engage with his mentors at home about his poetic techniques and defend his work, as he does to Marsh in August 1916:

> You know the conditions I have always worked under, and particularly with this last lot of poems. You know how earnestly one must wait on ideas, (you cannot coax real ones to you) and let as it were, a skin grow naturally round and through them. If you are not free, you can only, when the ideas come hot, seize them with the skin in tatters raw, crude, in some parts beautiful in others monstrous. Why print it then? Because those rare parts must not be lost. I work more and more as I write into more depth and lucidity, I am sure... If I could get a few months after the war to work and absorb myself completely into the thing, I'd write a great thing.
>
> I am enclosing a poem I wrote in the trenches, which is surely as simple as ordinary talk. You might object to the second line as vague, but that was the best way I could express the sense of dawn.

The poem was 'Break of Day in the Trenches', where the 'queer sardonic rat' runs between the 'strong eyes, fine limbs, haughty athletes' of the human beings on either side of the lines. The rat's mocking presence enables Rosenberg to draw out the complexities of the moral position, as the rat observes the 'athletes', while the poet, sticking a poppy behind his ear, considers the rat. The rat does not have the last word, for the poppy, though damaged, ends the poem:

> Poppies whose roots are in men's veins
> Drop, and are ever dropping;
> But mine in my ear is safe –
> Just a little white with the dust.

The poppy bears the 'dust' of the poet's own mortality – safe, but only for the moment.

In April 1917 Rosenberg told Marsh how pleased he was that he, Marsh, was buying more copies of his pamphlet *Moses*:

But it greatly pleases me, none the less, that this child of my brain should be seen and perhaps his beauties be discovered. His creator is in sadder plight; the harsh and unlovely times have made his mistress, the flighty Muse, abscond and elope with luckier rivals, but surely I shall hunt her and chase her somewhere into the summer and sweeter times.

Perhaps because of his persistent ill-health and his anxious family soliciting Marsh's help in lobbying the authorities, early in 1917 Rosenberg was transferred to a works unit of the Royal Engineers, and at the end of March the whole division was sent behind the lines to work on roads and railways. With the spring thaw the Germans retreated to the Hindenberg Line; the Canadians in the north took Vimy Ridge, and the 40th Division moved tentatively forward into the old German-held territory. But by the summer the advance had petered out and the Division ruefully named itself the 'Forgotten Fortieth'.

Sometime during that uneasy spring and summer Rosenberg wrote 'Returning, We Hear the Larks' and sent a copy to John Rodker. This short poem with its vivid sense of a particular transcendent moment in the dull and dangerous routine of the trenches, the recognition of the inextricable blending of peril and beauty of which war is only one aspect, shows how freely his imagination now dominated and used every part of his experience. Other war poets of course had noticed the amazing resilience of the shattered countryside, and the singing larks above the battlefield were, like the poppies, a recognized image of the absurdity of war. But for Rosenberg this is too commonplace a perception on its own, and as always he relates his images to a broader context than the battlefield; they become the focus for an examination of the power and danger of beauty. The night patrol returns to camp exhausted and looking forward to 'a little safe sleep':

> But hark! joy – joy – strange joy.
> Lo! heights of night ringing with unseen larks.
> Music showering our upturned list'ning faces.

Death could drop from the dark
As easily as song –
But song only dropped,
Like a blind man's dreams on the sand
By dangerous tides,
Like a girl's dark hair for she dreams no ruin lies there,
Or her kisses where a serpent hides.

In the other poems such as 'Daughters of War' and the verse plays he was struggling with at this time, the abstruseness of his images and his knotted language arise from the endeavour to concentrate on and follow through all elements of the experience. In 'Returning, We Hear the Larks' his aim is now for lucidity and the language is less clotted, but the fierce awareness of all possibilities suggested by the experience remains the controlling power of the poem. He wrote to Marsh in July 1917, 'I think with you that poetry should be definite thought and clear expression, however subtle; I don't think there should be any vagueness at all; but a sense of something hidden and felt to be there'.

During this last summer of his life he was again working with great concentration, in spite of the dangers and oppressive daily difficulties of his situation. In July he explained these to Sydney Schiff (who had himself sent Rosenberg a rather depressed letter):

> …things are so tumultuous and disturbing that unless one has everything handy, like an addressed envelope a pencil and a moment to spare one cannot write letters. One's envelopes get stuck and useless with the damp and you cannot replace them. I managed to jot down some ideas for poems now and then but I won['t send them to you because they are actual transcripts of the battlefield and you won['t like that, anyway just now.

One of these was the poem now acknowledged to be his greatest – 'Dead Man's Dump' – which he had written earlier in the summer; it is signed and dated 17 May 1917. He had found then that with the coming of summer physical discomfort eased a little, and his imagination too unfroze:

We are camping in the woods now and living great. My feet are almost healed now and my list of complaints has dwindled down to almost invisibility. I've written some lines suggested by going out wiring, or rather carrying wire up the line on limbers and running over dead bodies lying about. I don't think what I've written is very good but I think the substance is, and when I work on it I'll make it fine.

[Letter to Marsh, May 1917]

In the first three stanzas Rosenberg commits to the physical look and feel of the battlefield, and this time presents himself as an active participant, 'the bones crunched' under him, physically and emotionally:

> Their shut mouths made no moan,
> They lie there huddled, friend and foeman,
> Man born of man, and born of woman,
> And shells go crying over them
> From night till night and now.

With the third stanza the frantic and terrible activity of the battle-field is measured against the ageless power of the earth. Whereas for poets like Edmund Blunden, Edward Thomas and Wilfred Owen the natural world usually represents peace, beauty and normality, for Rosenberg the earth seems to take on some of the jealous devouring power of the 'God' and 'Female God' he evokes in other poems. Rosenberg asserts the human value of the destroyed life, not like Owen by mourning the beauty of men deformed by death, but characteristically by celebrating the energy of 'their dark souls':

> What fierce imaginings their dark souls lit
> Earth! have they gone into you?
> Somewhere they must have gone,
> And flung on your hard back
> Is their souls' sack,
> Emptied of God-ancestralled essences.
> Who hurled them out? Who hurled?

Owen's 'pity of war' is for Rosenberg not adequate to the enormity of the occurrence, but the lack of pathos and the vitality of the 'dark souls' are matched by the dynamic movement of the language, and give the dead a stature that overrides even the final irony – that it is fellow men who have 'hurled' away their lives. Rosenberg responds too strongly to the charged moment for easy grieving; he cannot offer consolation, but the vital movement of the language in the next stanza is itself informed with a tenderness that stands against the closure of death:

> None saw their spirits' shadow shake the grass,
> Or stood aside for the half used life to pass
> Out of those doomed nostrils and the doomed mouth,
> When the swift iron burning bee
> Drained the wild honey of their youth.

The next three stanzas interrupt the timeless dimension of the dead with a return to the violence and acute sense of borrowed time felt by the living, especially the poet aware of the 'startled blood' in his veins. The ninth stanza refocuses on a particular brutal death presented without explicit comment – it is the soul not the body which is significant:

> A man's brains splattered on
> A stretcher-bearer's face;
> His shook shoulders slipped their load,
> But when they bent to look again
> The drowning soul was sunk too deep
> For human tenderness.

Even so, the tenderness is there still, and moves from 'this dead' to the others:

> They left this dead with the older dead,
> Stretched at the cross roads.
> Burnt black by strange decay,
> Their sinister faces lie

The lid over each eye,
The grass and covered clay
More motion have than they,
Joined to the great sunk silences.

There is the silence of death, of history – 'the older dead' – of life without these lives, the silence of those who are left and reading the poem, confronting this. The delicate precision of 'the lid over each eye' shows Rosenberg making the exact techniques of the first Romantic poets his own; the firm rhythm and alliteration recall Wordsworth's 'A slumber did my spirit seal':

No motion has she now, no force;
She neither hears nor sees;
Rolled round in earth's diurnal course,
With rocks, and stones, and trees.

The Romantics' view of a natural universe quickened with divine and human power was now no longer a presence in Rosenberg's work. Once again he stands aside from that tradition in which the other war poets (and the Georgians) were still writing. His rejection of pity and the consolations of elegy is clear in the final two stanzas where again he moves from general contemplation to engagement with an individual consciousness, a dying soldier:

Here is one not long dead;
His dark hearing caught our far wheels,
And the choked soul stretched weak hands
To reach the living word the far wheels said,
The blood-dazed intelligence beating for light,
Crying through the suspense of the far torturing wheels
Swift for the end to break,
Or the wheels to break,
Cried as the tide of the world broke over his sight.

The poem ends as it began, with the limber crushing the dead – 'And our wheels grazed his dead face.'

In September 1917 Rosenberg came home for a final ten days' leave. Like many of his fellow soldiers he found the experience tense and difficult:

I am afraid I can do no writing or reading; I feel so restless here and un-anchored. We have lived in such an elemental way so long, things here don't look quite right to me somehow; or it may be the consciousness of my so limited time here for freedom – so little time to do so many things bewilders me.
[Letter to Gordon Bottomley, 21 September 1917]

That same month Edward Marsh's volume of *Georgian Poetry* was published, including the small extract from Rosenberg's *Moses*. In October Rosenberg was back in hospital with influenza – an early case of the epidemic that would devastate Europe the following year. Once more in the trenches in early 1918 he wrote sadly to Bottomley that, 'since I left the hospital all the poetry has gone quite out of me'.

He managed, however, to continue his letters to his family and to most of his regular correspondents, as if his longing for talk of books and poetry had only intensified as the pace of war quickened. Then, in the aftermath of the Somme battles, Rosenberg's battalion, the 11th King's Own Royal Lancasters, was decimated and broken up and Rosenberg was transferred to the 1st Battalion, from where he wrote to John Rodker (who was in a penal settlement for conscientious objectors) in early March 1918:

I hope you still keep the same good spirits of your last letter and that the work is not beyond your strength. My work is but somehow we blunder through. From hospital I went back to the line and we had a rough time with the mud. Balzac could give you the huge and terrible sensations of sinking in the mud. I was in the trenches a month when our Batt broke up and I am now in another Batt of our regiment...Just now we're out for a rest and I hope the warmer weather sets in when we go up the line again. It is quite impossible to write or think of writing stuff now, so I can only hope for hospital or the end of the war if I want to write.

The 1st Battalion went up to Arras on 11 March 1918. Before moving off Rosenberg had been able to meet his brother David, serving with the Tanks, who had been wounded and was himself just out of hospital. Possibly because he thought a hotter climate would improve his health, Rosenberg had been trying for a transfer to the Jewish Battalion, then stationed in Mesopotamia. Whether it was the thought of possibly being posted to the ancient Biblical lands, or an emotional longing for home and a return to the comforting memories of childhood, his last three poems concentrated on Old Testament themes. In two – 'The Burning of the Temple' and 'The Destruction of Jerusalem by the Babylonian Hordes' – he presents the violence of war as a force which had always been part of man's history and experience. On 19 March the battalion moved into the line, and by 28 March it was back in the reserve trenches for four days. Rosenberg had just time to answer Marsh's letter and enclose his third and last poem, 'Through these pale cold days':

> It[']s really my being lucky enough to bag an inch of candle that incites me to this pitch of punctual epistolary [*sic*]. I must measure my letter by the light…I've heard nothing further about the J[ewish] B[attalion]…but when we leave the trenches, I'll enquire further.…I wanted to write a battle song for the Judaens [*sic*] but can think of nothing strong and wonderful enough yet. Here's just a slight thing…I've seen no poetry for ages now so you mustn't be too critical – My vocabulary small enough before is impoverished and bare.

That same day, the Germans launched a full-scale attack. One entire battalion in Rosenberg's brigade was wiped out. The 1st King's Own went back into the line that day with a loss of seventy men. Day and night they crouched in the trenches under heavy artillery bombardment. Patrols went out each night to repair wire, and on the night of 31 March Rosenberg was detailed to join one. By the next day, it was clear he was not going to return. The remains of the patrol were later found, and Rosenberg is buried with his comrades in Bailleul East war cemetery, north-east of Arras, where each spring the skylarks still sing above his grave.

Rosenberg never committed himself wholly to any cause other than his own pursuit of art and poetry. His poverty, education and background made him an outsider, yet it was just that experience which equipped him to cope with the unforeseen horror of war in the trenches, and make cool and sophisticated use of it as an artist:

> I am determined that this war, with all its powers for devastation, shall not master my poeting; that is, if I am lucky enough to come through all right. I will not leave a corner of my consciousness covered up, but saturate myself with the strange and extraordinary new conditions of this life, and it will all refine itself into poetry later on.'
> [Letter to Laurence Binyon, Autumn 1916]

His war poems are strikingly different from those of his fellow poets because of his capacity to embrace and transmute 'the strange and extraordinary conditions' of trench life without the emotional recoil from the horrors of war which other major war poets such as Sassoon and Owen had to deal with. For Rosenberg, the shattering of a Christian civilization which so affects Owen for example, was not such a shock; as a Jewish immigrant from the East End of London who had already had to struggle for his education and the space to exercise his art he had fewer ideals to lose. He was a private soldier, coping with the physical squalor as well as the dangers of the trenches, while virtually all of his fellow poets were officers. The advantages officer status conferred were small but significant: a dugout rather than an open trench, and pen, paper and light to write by. What is remarkable about Rosenberg's work is its ambition, its largeness of vision, combined with its painterly, sensuous response to physical detail, splendid or sordid. These elements gave his work its durable originality and strength.

However, during the war years and their immediate aftermath the public turned to Rupert Brooke, the epitome of the glamorous soldier poet. After the war a reaction set in and readers and critics increasingly preferred the poems of Siegfried Sassoon and Wilfred Owen. These expressed a more straightforward antipathy to war than did the work of Rosenberg. Sassoon's and Owen's poetry was more finished, while Rosenberg's style was more erratic, more ambitious and less accessible. To a literary world committed to a Modernist poetry that was spare, intellectual and rigorous, Rosenberg's richness of language often seemed lush, old-fashioned and limited, although his poetry interested such influential figures as T. S. Eliot, Robert Graves, F. R. Leavis and D. W. Harding, later his editor along with Gordon Bottomley. Poets of the Second World War like Keith Douglas also rediscovered him: 'Rosenberg I only repeat what you were saying' ('Desert Flowers'). In recent years with the waning of Modernism's iron grip there has been a resurgence of interest in poets of the First World War, and gradually Rosenberg's work has claimed a widening share of critical attention in the USA and in Britain. What would probably please him more, however, is the increasing number of his poems included in anthologies. Every critic sees him in terms of dichotomies, but each sees a different dichotomy. He is English but Jewish; he is from London's East End yet also from the Slade School and the Café Royal; his work reveals Hebrew elements as well as his relationship to the English Romantic tradition; he is orthodox and unorthodox in his religious vision; from a pacifist background, he is nonetheless obsessed with the creative and destructive energy of power. These dichotomies provide the tension intrinsic to his poetry's strength but they also generate a quality that goes beyond this kind of analysis. He and his poetry became the touchstone of cultural conflicts that revealed themselves only after his death.

These conflicts can be found not only within his poetry but also in his personality and social predicament. Rosenberg, who always felt himself to be on the periphery of mainstream society, has become important now that that very periphery has come to be seen as a crucial area of social and cultural change. Similarly, his working-class status and Jewishness, both thought disadvantageous to him in his lifetime, have become central concerns today. As an artist he stood aside from the mainstream traditions, and this gives him significance in the present age, with its increasing tendency to question traditions. Rosenberg was a victim several times over, of his own poverty and rootlessness, of the social structure, of established cultural attitudes, and finally of the war itself. Yet against all the odds he never gave up, either as a soldier or as a poet.

This constancy was the source both of his failure and of his ultimate success. The resonance and poignancy of his poetry transcends the brief facts of his life history and the incompleteness of his work. Rosenberg's poetic ability to confront and transform alienation and difficulty, and his unique artistic gift for turning defeats into victories, have confirmed his international stature as a major poet of the First World War and have made his life and work increasingly significant for our own times.

JEAN P. LIDDIARD
April 2003

ACKNOWLEDGEMENTS

Isaac Rosenberg's reputation as an important artistic figure of the First World War has grown considerably since his death in 1918, and much of the credit for this must go to the Rosenberg family and its descendants, especially his sister Annie Wynick and his nephew Isaac Horvitch. Sadly much of Rosenberg's original work has disappeared over the years, but the family and his literary executors and mentors kept many of his manuscripts, letters, drawings and paintings together until a permanent place was found for them at the British Museum, the British Library and the Imperial War Museum. Rosenberg's growing number of admirers owe them a debt of gratitude for this, and for the generosity with which the family has made the material available. The Imperial War Museum in particular has done a great deal to promote Rosenberg's work over the years, and my thanks are due especially to the director Robert Crawford, and to Angela Godwin, Christopher Dowling, Roderick Suddaby and Elizabeth Bowers.

Anne Harvey made possible the Rosenberg poetry reading I compiled for the National Portrait Gallery, which was splendidly performed by the actor Sam Dastor. Clive Bettington also gave us the opportunity to present it at the Jewish Cultural Festival in Whitechapel. I am deeply grateful to all three of them for their encouragement and support in bringing Rosenberg's life and work to a wider public. Anne Harvey also introduced me to Stephen Stuart-Smith of Enitharmon Press; Rosenberg and I could have had no better publisher.

I must acknowledge the unfailing help, both professional and personal, of my friend Erika Langmuir, and – over many years – the deep and constant personal support, as well as the interest and advice, of my husband, Michael Collinson.

POEMS

DAWN BEHIND NIGHT

Lips! bold, frenzied utterance, shape to the thoughts that are
    prompted by hate
Of the red streaming burden of wrong we have borne and still bear;
That wealth with its soul-crushing scourges placed into its hands by
    fate,
Hath made the cement of its towers, grim-girdled by our despair.

Should it die in the death that they make, in the silence that follows
    the sob;
In the voiceless depth of the waters that closes upon our grief;
Who shall know of the bleakness assigned us for the fruits that we
    reap and they rob?
To pour out the strong wine of pity, outstretch the kind hand in
    relief.

In the golden glare of the morning, in the solemn serene of the night,
We look on each other's faces, and we turn to our prison bar;
In pitiless travail of toil and outside the precious light,
What wonder we know not our manhood in the curse of the things
    that are?

In the life or the death they dole us from the rags and the bones of
    their store,
In the blood they feed but to drink of, in the pity they feign in their
    pride,
Lies the glimpse of a heaven behind it, for the ship hath left the
    shore,
That will find us and free us and take us where its portals are opened
    wide.

1909

'THE WORLD RUMBLES BY ME'

The world rumbles by me – can I heed?
The rose it is crimson – and I bleed.

The rose of my heart glows deep afar;
And I grope in the darkness 'twixt star and star.

Only in night grows the flower of peace,
Spreading its odours of rest and ease.

It dies in the day like light in the night.
It revives like tears in the eyes of delight.

For the youth at my heart beats wild and loud;
And raves in my ear of a girl and a shroud.

Of a golden girl with the soul in her eyes,
To teach me love and to make me wise.

With the fire on her lips and the wine in her hands,
To bind me strong in her silken bands.

For time and fate are striding to meet
One unseen with soundless feet.

The world rustles by me – let me heed.
Clutched in its madness till I bleed.

For the rose of my heart glows deep afar.
If I stretch my hand, I may clasp a star.

1911

44

'GOD LOOKED CLEAR AT ME THROUGH HER EYES'

God looked clear at me through her eyes,
And when her fresh and sweet lips spake,
Through dawn-flushed gates of Paradise
Such silvern birds did wing and shake

God's fervent music on my soul,
And with their jewelled quivering feet
Did rend apart the quiet stole
That shades from girl-fanned pulsing heat.

Upon a gold branch in my breast
They made their nest, while sweet and warm
Hung wav'ring thoughts like rose-leaves drest;
My soul the sky to keep from harm.

In the heart's woods mysterious
Where feelings lie remote and far,
They fly with touch imperious,
And loose emotion's hidden bar.

And to dark pools of brooding care,
And blinding wastes of loneliness,
They gleam a Paradisal air,
And warm with a divine caress.

1912

'NOW THE SPIRIT'S SONG HAS WITHERED'

Now the spirit's song has withered
As a song of last year's June
That has made the air its tomb.
Shall we ever find it after
Sighing in some summer tune
That is sealèd now in gloom,
Safe for light and laughter?

Now the sky blooms full of colour,
Houses glow and windows shine
Glittering with impatient wings.
Where they go to may I follow
Since mine eyes have made them mine?
Shall I ever find these things
Hid in hill or hollow?

1911–12

PEACE

Where the dreamy mountains brood
Ever in their ancient mood
Would I go and dream with them
Till I graft me on their stem.

With fierce energy I aspire
To be thát the Gods desire
As the dreamy mountains are
And no God can break or mar.

Soon the world shall fade and be
One with still eternity
As the dreamy hills that lie
Silent to the passing sky.

1912

DON JUAN'S SONG

The moon is in an ecstasy,
It wanes not nor can grow.
The heavens are in a mist of love,
And deepest knowledge know.
What things in nature seem to move
Bear love as I bear love?
And bear my pleasures so?

The moon will fade when morning comes,
The heavens will dream no more.
In our missed meetings are eyes hard?
What shadows fleck the door
Averted, when we part? What guard
Scents death in each vain word?
What haggard haunts the shore?

I bear my love as streams that bear
The sky still flow or shake.
Though deep within too far on high.
Light blossoms kiss and wake
The waters sooner than the sky.
And if they kiss and die!
God made them frail to break.

'EVEN NOW YOUR EYES ARE MIXED IN MINE'

Even now your eyes are mixed in mine.
I see you not, but surely, he –
This stricken gaze, has looked on thee.
From him your glances shine.

Even now I felt your hand in mine.
This breeze that warms my open palm
Has surely kist yours; such thrilled calm
No lull can disentwine.

The words you spoke just now, how sweet!
These grasses heard and bend to tell.
The green grows pale your speech to spell,
How its green heart must beat!

I breathe you. Here the air enfolds
Your absent presence, as fire cleaves,
Leaving the places warm it leaves.
Such warmth a warm word holds.

Bruised are our words and our full thought
Breaks like dull rain from some rich cloud.
Our pulses leap alive and proud.
Colour, not heat, is caught.

extract from DAY
(from NIGHT AND DAY)

One night and one day and what sang Desire?
All that God sings betwixt them is not lost.
One night and one day, what did Beauty choir?
If our souls hearken little is the most,
And nothing is which is not living sound,
All flowing with the eternal harmony
That with creation's first day was unwound.
One night and one day – what sang Hope to me?
That the next night and day love's song must fill.
He showed me in a mirror, ecstasy,
And a new dawn break over the old hill.

Twilight's wide eyes are mystical
With some far off knowledge;
Secret is the mouth of her,
And secret her eyes.

Lo! she braideth her hair
Of dim soft purple and thread of satin.
Lo! she flasheth her hand –
Her hand of pearl and silver in shadow.
Slowly she braideth her hair
Over her glimmering eyes,
Floating her ambient robes
Over the trees and the skies,
Over the wind-footing grass.
Softly she braideth her hair
With shadow deeper than thought.

To make her comely for night?
To make her meet for the night?

Slowly she heaveth her breast,
For the night to lie there and rest?

Hush, her eyes are in trance
Swooningly raised to the sky.
What heareth she so to enthral?
Filleth her sight to amaze?

'From the sweet gardens of the sky
Whose roots are pleasures under earth,
Whose atmosphere is melody
To hail each deathless minute's birth,
Between frail night and frailer day
I sing what soon the moon will say,
And what the sun has said in mirth.

'I sing the centre of all bliss.
The peace like a sweet-smelling tree
That spreads its perfumed holiness
In unperturbed serenity.
Between the darkness and the light,
I hang above my message bright
The clamour of mortality.

'Here, from the bowers of Paradise
Whose flowers from deep contentment grew,
To reach his hand out to the wise
My casement God's bright eyes look through.
For him whose eyes do look for Him
He leans out through the seraphim
And His own bosom draws him to.'

I heard the evening start.

[1912 and earlier]

ASPIRATION

The roots of a dead universe are shrunken in my brain;
And the tinsel leafed branches of the charred trees are strewn;
And the chaff we deem'd for harvest shall be turned to golden grain,
While May no more will mimic March, but June be only June.

Lo! a ghost enleaguer'd city where no ghostly footfall came!
And a rose within the mirror with the fragrance of it hid;
And mine ear prest to the mouth of the shadow of a name;
But no ghost or speech or fragrance breathing on my faint eyelid.

I would crash the city's ramparts, touch the ghostly hands without.
Break the mirror, feel the scented warm lit petals of the rose.
Would mine ears be stretched for shadows in the fading of the
    doubt?
Other ears shall wait my shadow, – can you see behind the brows?

For I would see with mine own eyes the glory and the gold.
With a strange and fervid vision see the glamour and the dream.
And chant an incantation in a measure new and bold,
And enaureole a glory round an unawaken'd theme.

                                                                    1912

HEART'S FIRST WORD
(I)

To sweeten a swift minute so
With such rare fragrance of sweet speech,
And make the after hours go
In a blank yearning each on each;
To drain the springs till they be dry,
And then in anguish thirst for drink,
So but to glimpse her robe thirst I,
And my soul hungers and I sink.

There is no word that we have said
Whereby the lips and heart are fire;
No look the linkèd glances read
That held the springs of deep desire.
And yet the sounds her glad lips gave
Are on my soul vibrating still.
Her eyes that swept me as a wave
Shine my soul's worship to fulfil.

Her hair, her eyes, her throat and chin;
Sweet hair, sweet eyes, sweet throat, so sweet,
So fair because the ways of sin
Have never known her perfect feet.
By what far ways and marvellous
May I such lovely heaven reach?
What dread dark seas and perilous
Lie 'twixt love's silence and love's speech?

1911–12

THE POET
(II)

He takes the glory from the gold
For consecration of the mould,
He strains his ears to the clouds' lips,
He sings the song they sang to him
And his brow dips
In amber that the seraphim
Have held for him and hold.

So shut in are our lives, so still,
That we see not of good or ill –
A dead world since ourselves are dead.
Till he, the master, speaks and lo!
The dead world's shed,
Strange winds, new skies and rivers flow
Illumined from the hill.

SONG

A silver rose to show
Is your sweet face,
And like the heavens' white brow,
Sometime God's battle place,
Your blood is quiet now.

Your body is a star
Unto my thought.
But stars are not too far
And can be caught –
Small pools their prisons are.

'HAVE WE SAILED AND HAVE WE WANDERED'

Have we sailed and have we wandered,
Still beyond, the hills are blue.
Have we spent and have we squandered,
What's before us still is new.

See the foam of unheard waters
And the gleam of hidden skies,
Footsteps of Eve's whiter daughters
Flash between our dreaming eyes.

Soundless waning to the spirit,
Still – O still the hills are blue,
Ever and yet never near it,
There where our far childhood grew.

1914

DAWN

O tender, first cold flush of rose,
O budded dawn, wake dreamily;
Your dim lips as your lids unclose
Murmur your own sad threnody.
O as the soft and frail lights break
Upon your eyelids, and your eyes
Wider and wider grow and wake,
The old pale glory dies.

And then, as sleep lays down to sleep
And all her dreams lie somewhere dead,
(While naked day digs goldly deep
For light to lie uncovered),
Your own ghost fades with dream-ghosts there,
Our lorn eyes see mid glimmering lips,
Pass through the haunted dream-moved air,
Slowly, their laden ships.

1914

THE FEMALE GOD

We curl into your eyes.
They drink our fires and have never drained.
In the fierce forest of your hair
Our desires beat blindly for their treasure.

In your eyes' subtle pit
Far down, glimmer our souls.
And your hair like massive forest trees
Shadows our pulses, overtired and dumb.

Like a candle lost in an electric glare
Our spirits tread your eyes' infinities.
In the wrecking waves of your tumultuous locks
Do you not hear the moaning of our pulses?

Queen! Goddess! animal!
In sleep do your dreams battle with our souls?
When your hair is spread like a lover on the pillow,
Do not our jealous pulses wake between?

You have dethroned the ancient God.
You have usurped his sabbath, his common days,
Yea! every moment is delivered to you.
Our Temple, our Eternal, our one God.

Our souls have passed into your eyes
Our days into your hair.
And you, our rose-deaf prison, are very pleased with the world.
Your world.

1914

'SUMMER'S LIPS ARE AGLOW'

Summer's lips are aglow, afresh
For our old lips to kiss,
The tingling of the flesh
Makes life aware of this.

Whose eyes are wild with love?
Whose hair a blowing flame
I feel around and above
Laughing my dreams to shame?

My dreams like stars gone out
Were blossoms for your day;
Red flower of mine I will shout,
I have put my dreams away.

                                    1914–15

'I AM THE BLOOD'

I am the blood
Streaming the veins of sweetness; sharp and sweet,
Beauty has pricked the live veins of my soul
And sucked all being in.

I am the air
Prowling the room of beauty, climbing her soft
Walls of surmise, her ceilings that close in.
She breathes me as her breath.

I am the death
Whose monument is beauty, and forever
Although I lie unshrouded in life's tomb,
She is my cenotaph.

ON RECEIVING NEWS OF THE WAR

Snow is a strange white word;
No ice or frost
Have asked of bud or bird
For Winter's cost.

Yet ice and frost and snow
From earth to sky
This Summer land doth know,
No man knows why.

In all men's hearts it is.
Some spirit old
Hath turned with malign kiss
Our lives to mould.

Red fangs have torn His face.
God's blood is shed.
He mourns from His lone place
His children dead.

O! ancient crimson curse!
Corrode, consume.
Give back this universe
Its pristine bloom.

Cape Town, 1914

A GIRL'S THOUGHTS

Dim apprehension of a trust
Comes over me this quiet hour,
As though the silence were a flower,
And this, its perfume, dark like dust.

My individual self would cling
Through fear, through pride, unto its fears.
It strives to shut out what it hears,
The founts of being, murmuring.

O! need, whose hauntings terrorize;
Whether my maiden ways would hide,
Or lose, and to that need subside,
Life shrinks, and instinct dreads surprise.

1914

WEDDED

(I)

They leave their love-lorn haunts,
Their sigh-warm floating Eden;
And they are mute at once;
Mortals by God unheeden;
By their past kisses chidden.

But they have kist and known
Clear things we dim by guesses –
Spirit to spirit grown –
Heaven, born in hand caresses –
Love, fall from sheltering tresses.

And they are dumb and strange;
Bared trees bowed from each other.
Their last green interchange
What lost dreams shall discover?
Dead, strayed, to love-stranged lover.

WEDDED
(II)

The knotted moment that untwists
Into the narrow laws of love,
Its ends are rolled round our four wrists
That once could stretch and rove.

See our confined fingers stray
O'er delicate fibres that recoil,
And blushing hints as cold as clay;
Love is tired after toil.

But hush! two twin moods meet in air;
Two spirits of one gendered thought.
Our chained hands loosened everywhere
Kindness like death's have caught.

MIDSUMMER FROST
(1)

A July ghost, aghast at the strange winter,
Wonders, at burning noon, (all summer seeming),
How, like a sad thought buried in light words,
Winter, an alien presence, is ambushed here.
See, from the fire-fountained noon there creep
Lazy yellow ardours towards pale evening,
Dragging the sun across the shell of thought.
A web threaded with fading fire.
Futile and fragile lure!
All July walks her floors that roof this ice,
My frozen heart the summer cannot reach,
Hidden as a root from air, or star from day.
A frozen pool whereon mirth dances
Where the shining boys would fish.

Amorous to woo the golden kissing sun,
Your flaunting green hoods bachic eyes
And flower-flinging hands,
Show quaint as in some frolic masker's whim,
Or painted ruby on a dead white rose.
Deriding those blind who slinked past God
And their untasked inheritance,
(Whose sealed eyes trouble not the sun)
With a thought of Maytime once,
And Maytime dances;
Of a dim pearl-faery boat
And golden glimmerings;
Waving white hands that ripple lakes of sadness
Until the sadness vanishes and the stagnant pool remains.

65

Pitiless I am, for I bind thee, laughter's apostle,
Even as thy garland's glance, and thy soul is merry, to see
How in night-hanging forest of eating maladies,
A frozen forest of moon-unquiet madness
The moon-drunk, haunted, pierced soul, dies.
Tarnished and arid, dead before it dies.
Starved by its Babel folly, stark it lies,
Stabbed by life's jealous eyes.

1914

MIDSUMMER FROST
(II)

A July ghost, aghast at the strange winter,
Wonders, at burning noon, (all summer seeming),
How, like a sad thought buried in light words,
Winter, an alien presence, is ambushed here.

See, from the fire-fountained noon there creep
Lazy yellow ardours towards pale evening,
To thread dark and vain fire
Over my unsens'd heart,
Dead heart, no urgent summer can reach.
Hidden as a root from air or a star from day;
A frozen pool whereon mirth dances;
Where the shining boys would fish.

My blinded brain pierced is,
And searched by a thought, and pangful
With bitter ooze of a joyous knowledge
Of some starred time outworn.
Like blind eyes that have slinked past God,
And light, their untasked inheritance,
(Sealed eyes that trouble never the Sun)
Yet has feel of a Maytime pierced.
He heareth the Maytime dances;
Frees from their airy prison, bright voices,
To loosen them in his dark imagination,
Powered with girl revels rare
And silks and merry colours,
And all the unpeopled ghosts that walk in words.
Till wave white hands that ripple lakes of sadness,
Until the sadness vanishes and the stagnant pool remains.

Underneath this summer air can July dream
How, in night-hanging forest of eating maladies,
A frozen forest of moon unquiet madness,
The moon-drunk haunted pierced soul dies;
Starved by its Babel folly, lying stark,
Unvexed by July's warm eyes.

1914–15

IF YOU ARE FIRE

If you are fire and I am fire,
Who blows the flame apart
So that desire eludes desire
Around one central heart?

A single root and separate bough,
And what blind hands between
That make our longing's mutual glow
As if it had not been?

BREAK IN BY SUBTLER WAYS

Break in by subtler nearer ways;
Dulled closeness is too far.
And separate we are
Through joined days.

The shine and strange romance of time
In absence hides and change.
Shut eyes and hear the strange
Perfect new chime.

THE ONE LOST

I mingle with your bones.
You steal in subtle noose
This lighted dust Jehovah loans
And now I lose.

What will the Lender say
When I shall not be found,
Safe sheltered at the Judgment Day,
Being in you bound?

He'll hunt thronged wards of Heaven,
Call to uncoffined earth
'Where is this soul unjudged, not given
Dole for good's dearth?'

And I, lying so safe
Within you, hearing all,
To have cheated God shall laugh,
Freed by your thrall.

THE DEAD HEROES

Flame out, you glorious skies,
Welcome our brave,
Kiss their exultant eyes;
Give what they gave.

Flash, mailed seraphim,
Your burning spears;
New days to outflame their dim
Heroic years.

Thrills their baptismal tread
The bright proud air;
The embattled plumes outspread
Burn upwards there.

Flame out, flame out, O Song!
Star ring to star,
Strong as our hurt is strong
Our children are.

Their blood is England's heart;
By their dead hands
It is their noble part
That England stands.

England – Time gave them thee;
They gave back this
To win Eternity
And claim God's kiss.

1914

THE CLOISTER

Our eyes no longer sail the tidal streets,
Nor harbour where the hours like petals float
By sensual treasures glittering through thin walls
Of women's eyes and colour's mystery.

The roots of our eternal souls were fed
On the world's dung and now their blossoms gleam.
God gives to glisten in an angel's hair
These He has gardened, for they please His eyes.

EXPRESSION

Call – call – and bruise the air:
Shatter dumb space!
Yea! We will fling this passion everywhere;
Leaving no place

For the superb and grave
Magnificent throng,
The pregnant queens of quietness that brave
And edge our song

Of wonder at the light,
(Our life-leased home),
Of greeting to our housemates. And in might
Our song shall roam

Life's heart, a blossoming fire
Blown bright by thought,
While gleams and fades the infinite desire,
Phantasmed naught.

Can this be caught and caged?
Wings can be clipt
Of eagles, the sun's gaudy measure gauged,
But no sense dipt

In the mystery of sense:
The troubled throng
Of words break out like smother'd fire through dense
And smouldering wrong.

GOD

In his malodorous brain what slugs and mire,
Lanthorned in his oblique eyes, guttering burned!
His body lodged a rat where men nursed souls.
The world flashed grape-green eyes of a foiled cat
To him. On fragments of an old shrunk power,
On shy and maimed, on women wrung awry,
He lay, a bullying hulk, to crush them more.
But when one, fearless, turned and clawed like bronze,
Cringing was easy to blunt these stern paws,
And he would weigh the heavier on those after.

Who rests in God's mean flattery now? Your wealth
Is but his cunning to make death more hard.
Your iron sinews take more pain in breaking.
And he has made the market for your beauty
Too poor to buy, although you die to sell.
Only that he has never heard of sleep;
And when the cats come out the rats are sly.
Here we are safe till he slinks in at dawn.

But he has gnawed a fibre from strange roots,
And in the morning some pale wonder ceases.
Things are not strange and strange things are forgetful.
Ah! if the day were arid, somehow lost
Out of us, but it is as hair of us,
And only in the hush no wind stirs it.
And in the light vague trouble lifts and breathes,
And restlessness still shadows the lost ways.
The fingers shut on voices that pass through,
Where blind farewells are taken easily . . .

Ah! this miasma of a rotting God!

[1916 or earlier]

75

FIRST FRUIT

I did not pluck at all,
And I am sorry now.
The garden is not barred,
But the boughs are heavy with snow,
The flake-blossoms thickly fall,
And the hid roots sigh, 'How long will our flowers be marred?'

Strange as a bird were dumb,
Strange as a hueless leaf,
As one deaf hungers to hear
Or gazes without belief,
The fruit yearned 'fingers, come'.
O, shut hands, be empty another year.

[1915–16]

CHAGRIN

Caught still as Absalom,
Surely the air hangs
From the swayless cloud-boughs,
Like hair of Absalom
Caught and hanging still.

From the imagined weight
Of spaces in a sky
Of mute chagrin, my thoughts
Hang like branch-clung hair
To trunks of silence swung,
With the choked soul weighing down
Into thick emptiness.
Christ! end this hanging death,
For endlessness hangs therefrom.

Invisibly – branches break
From invisible trees –
The cloud-woods where we rush,
Our eyes holding so much,
Which we must ride dim ages round
Ere the hands (we dream) can touch,
We ride, we ride, before the morning
The secret roots of the sun to tread,
And suddenly
We are lifted of all we know
And hang from implacable boughs.
                              [1915–16]

MARCHING
(AS SEEN FROM THE LEFT FILE)

My eyes catch ruddy necks
Sturdily pressed back –
All a red brick moving glint.
Like flaming pendulums, hands
Swing across the khaki –
Mustard-coloured khaki –
To the automatic feet.
We husband the ancient glory
In these bared necks and hands.
Not broke is the forge of Mars;
But a subtler brain beats iron
To shoe the hoofs of death,
(Who paws dynamic air now).
Blind fingers loose an iron cloud
To rain immortal darkness
On strong eyes.

[1915–16]

SLEEP

Godhead's lip hangs
When our pulses have no golden tremours,
And his whips are flicked by mice
And all star-amorous things.

Drops, drops of shivering quiet
Filter under my lids.
Now only am I powerful.
What though the cunning gods outwit us here
In daytime and in playtime,
Surely they feel the gyves we lay on them
In our sleep.

O, subtle gods lying hidden!
O, gods with your oblique eyes!
Your elbows in the dawn, and wrists
Bright with the afternoon,

Do you not shake when a mortal slides
Into your own unvexed peace?
When a moving stillness breaks over your knees

(An emanation of piled aeons' pressure)
From our bodies flat and straight,
And your limbs are locked,
Futilely gods',
And shut your sinister essences?

[1915–16]

HEART'S FIRST WORD
(II)

And all her soft dark hair,
Breathed for him like a prayer.
And her white lost face,
Was prisoned to some far place.
Love was not denied –
Love's ends would hide.
And flower and fruit and tree
Were under its sea.
Yea! its abundance knelt
Where the nerves felt
The springs of feeling flow
And made pain grow.
There seemed no root or sky
But a pent infinity
Where apparitions dim
Sculptured each whim
In flame and wandering mist
Of kisses to be kist.

[1915–16]

'GREEN THOUGHTS ARE'

Green thoughts are
Ice block on a barrow
Gleaming in July.
A little boy with bare feet
And jewels at his nose stands by.

LUSITANIA

Chaos! that coincides with this militant purpose.
Chaos! the heart of this earnest malignancy.
Chaos! that helps, chaos that gives to shatter
Mind-wrought, mind-unimagining energies
For topless ill, of dynamite and iron.
Soulless logic, inventive enginery.
Now you have got the peace-faring *Lusitania*,
Germany's gift – all earth they would give thee,
   Chaos.

                    [?1915]

THE TROOP SHIP

Grotesque and queerly huddled
Contortionists to twist
The sleepy soul to a sleep,
We lie all sorts of ways
And cannot sleep.
The wet wind is so cold,
And the lurching men so careless,
That, should you drop to a doze,
Winds' fumble or men's feet
Are on your face.

1916

AUGUST 1914

What in our lives is burnt
In the fire of this?
The heart's dear granary?
The much we shall miss?

Three lives hath one life –
Iron, honey, gold.
The gold, the honey gone –
Left is the hard and cold.

Iron are our lives
Molten right through our youth.
A burnt space through ripe fields,
A fair mouth's broken tooth.

                              1916

THE JEW

Moses, from whose loins I sprung,
Lit by a lamp in his blood
Ten immutable rules, a moon
For mutable lampless men.

The blonde, the bronze, the ruddy,
With the same heaving blood,
Keep tide to the moon of Moses,
Then why do they sneer at me?

SPRING 1916

Slow, rigid, is this masquerade
That passes as through a difficult air;
Heavily – heavily passes.
What has she fed on? Who her table laid
Through the three seasons? What forbidden fare
Ruined her as a mortal lass is?

I played with her two years ago,
Who might be now her own sister in stone,
So altered from her May mien,
When round vague pink a necklace of warm snow
Laughed to her throat where my mouth's touch had gone.
How is this, ruined Queen?

Who lured her vivid beauty so
To be that strained chilled thing that moves
So ghastly midst her young brood
Of pregnant shoots that she for men did grow?
Where are the strong men who made these their loves?
Spring! God pity your mood.

1916

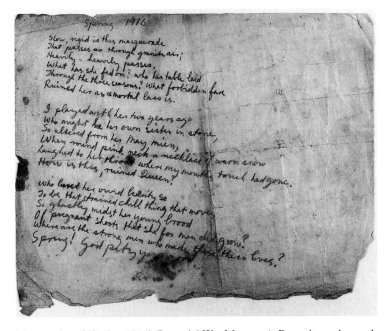

Manuscript of 'Spring 1916' (Imperial War Museum). Rosenberg changed 'pink neck' in line 10 to 'vague pink' in the printed version.

FROM FRANCE

The spirit drank the café lights;
All the hot life that glittered there,
And heard men say to women gay,
'Life is just so in France'.

The spirit dreams of café lights,
And golden faces and soft tones,
And hears men groan to broken men,
'This is not Life in France'.

Heaped stones and a charred signboard shows
With grass between and dead folk under,
And some birds sing, while the spirit takes wing.
And this is Life in France.

[1916]

IN THE TRENCHES

I snatched two poppies
From the parapet's ledge,
Two bright red poppies
That winked on the ledge.

Behind my ear
I stuck one through,
One blood red poppy
I gave to you.

The sandbags narrowed
And screwed out our jest,
And tore the poppy
You had on your breast . . .
Down – a shell – O! Christ,
I am choked . . . safe . . . dust blind, I
See trench floor poppies
Strewn. Smashed you lie.

1916

BREAK OF DAY IN THE TRENCHES

The darkness crumbles away.
It is the same old druid Time as ever,
Only a live thing leaps my hand,
A queer sardonic rat,
As I pull the parapet's poppy
To stick behind my ear.
Droll rat, they would shoot you if they knew
Your cosmopolitan sympathies.
Now you have touched this English hand
You will do the same to a German
Soon, no doubt, if it be your pleasure
To cross the sleeping green between.
It seems you inwardly grin as you pass
Strong eyes, fine limbs, haughty athletes,
Less chanced than you for life,
Bonds to the whims of murder,
Sprawled in the bowels of the earth,
The torn fields of France.
What do you see in our eyes
At the shrieking iron and flame
Hurled through still heavens?
What quaver – what heart aghast?
Poppies whose roots are in man's veins
Drop, and are ever dropping;
But mine in my ear is safe –
Just a little white with the dust.

June 1916

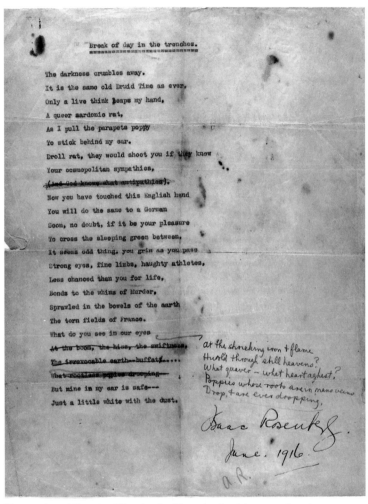

Typescript of 'Break of Day in the Trenches', with corrections in
Rosenberg's hand (Imperial War Museum).

HOME-THOUGHTS FROM FRANCE

Wan, fragile faces of joy!
Pitiful mouths that strive
To light with smiles the place
We dream we walk alive.

To you I stretch my hands,
Hands shut in pitiless trance
In the land of ruin and woe,
The desolate land of France.

Dear faces startled and shaken,
Out of wild dust and sounds
You yearn to me, lure and sadden
My heart with futile bounds.

'A WORM FED ON THE HEART OF CORINTH'

A worm fed on the heart of Corinth,
Babylon and Rome:
Not Paris raped tall Helen,
But this incestuous worm,
Who lured her vivid beauty
To his amorphous sleep.
England! famous as Helen
Is thy betrothal sung
To him the shadowless,
More amorous than Solomon.

1916

THE DYING SOLDIER

'Here are houses', he moaned,
'I could reach but my brain swims.'
Then they thundered and flashed
And shook the earth to its rims.

'They are gunpits', he gasped,
'Our men are at the guns.
Water – water – O water
For one of England's dying sons.'

'We cannot give you water,
Were all England in your breath,'
'Water! – water! – O water!'
He moaned and swooned to death.

IN WAR

Fret the nonchalant noon
With your spleen
Or your gay brow,
For the motion of your spirit
Ever moves with these.

When day shall be too quiet,
Deaf to you
And your dumb smile,
Untuned air shall lap the stillness
In the old space for your voice –

The voice that once could mirror
Remote depths
Of moving being,
Stirred by responsive voices near,
Suddenly stilled for ever.

No ghost darkens the places
Dark to One;
But my eyes dream,
And my heart is heavy to think
How it was heavy once.

In the old days when death
Stalked the world
For the flower of men,
And the rose of beauty faded
And pined in the great gloom,

One day we dug a grave:
We were vexed
With the sun's heat.
We scanned the hooded dead:
At noon we sat and talked.

How death had kissed their eyes
Three dread noons since,
How human art won
The dark soul to flicker
Till it was lost again:

And we whom chance kept whole –
But haggard,
Spent – were charged
To make a place for them who knew
No pain in any place.

The good priest came to pray;
Our ears half heard,
And half we thought
Of alien things, irrelevant;
And the heat and thirst were great.

The good priest read: 'I heard . . .'
Dimly my brain
Held words and lost . . .
Sudden my blood ran cold . . .
God! God! it could not be.

He read my brother's name;
I sank –
I clutched the priest
They did not tell me it was he
Was killed three days ago.

What are the great sceptred dooms
To us, caught
In the wild wave?
We break ourselves on them,
My brother, our hearts and years.

1917

THE IMMORTALS

I killed them, but they would not die.
Yea! all the day and all the night
For them I could not rest nor sleep,
Nor guard from them nor hide in flight.

Then in my agony I turned
And made my hands red in their gore.
In vain – for faster than I slew
They rose more cruel than before.

I killed and killed with slaughter mad;
I killed till all my strength was gone.
And still they rose to torture me,
For Devils only die in fun.

I used to think the Devil hid
In women's smiles and wine's carouse.
I called him Satan, Balzebub.
But now I call him, dirty louse.

1917

LOUSE HUNTING

Nudes – stark and glistening,
Yelling in lurid glee. Grinning faces
And raging limbs
Whirl over the floor one fire.
For a shirt verminously busy
Yon soldier tore from his throat, with oaths
Godhead might shrink at, but not the lice.
And soon the shirt was aflare
Over the candle he'd lit while we lay.

Then we all sprang up and stript
To hunt the verminous brood.
Soon like a demons' pantomime
The place was raging.
See the silhouettes agape,
See the gibbering shadows
Mixed with the battled arms on the wall.
See gargantuan hooked fingers
Pluck in supreme flesh
To smutch supreme littleness.
See the merry limbs in hot Highland fling
Because some wizard vermin
Charmed from the quiet this revel
When our ears were half lulled
By the dark music
Blown from Sleep's trumpet.

                                                1917

RETURNING, WE HEAR THE LARKS

Sombre the night is.
And though we have our lives, we know
What sinister threat lurks there.

Dragging these anguished limbs, we only know
This poison-blasted track opens on our camp –
On a little safe sleep.

But hark! joy – joy – strange joy.
Lo! heights of night ringing with unseen larks.
Music showering our upturned list'ning faces.

Death could drop from the dark
As easily as song –
But song only dropped,
Like a blind man's dreams on the sand
By dangerous tides,
Like a girl's dark hair for she dreams no ruin lies there,
Or her kisses where a serpent hides.

1917

DEAD MAN'S DUMP

The plunging limbers over the shattered track
Racketed with their rusty freight,
Stuck out like many crowns of thorns,
And the rusty stakes like sceptres old
To stay the flood of brutish men
Upon our brothers dear.

The wheels lurched over sprawled dead
But pained them not, though their bones crunched,
Their shut mouths made no moan,
They lie there huddled, friend and foeman,
Man born of man, and born of woman,
And shells go crying over them
From night till night and now.

Earth has waited for them
All the time of their growth
Fretting for their decay:
Now she has them at last!
In the strength of their strength
Suspended – stopped and held.

What fierce imaginings their dark souls lit
Earth! have they gone into you?
Somewhere they must have gone,
And flung on your hard back
Is their souls' sack,
Emptied of God-ancestralled essences.
Who hurled them out? Who hurled?

None saw their spirits' shadow shake the grass,
Or stood aside for the half used life to pass
Out of those doomed nostrils and the doomed mouth,
When the swift iron burning bee
Drained the wild honey of their youth.

What of us, who flung on the shrieking pyre,
Walk, our usual thoughts untouched,
Our lucky limbs as on ichor fed,
Immortal seeming ever?
Perhaps when the flames beat loud on us,
A fear may choke in our veins
And the startled blood may stop.

The air is loud with death,
The dark air spurts with fire
The explosions ceaseless are.
Timelessly now, some minutes past,
These dead strode time with vigorous life,
Till the shrapnel called 'an end!'
But not to all. In bleeding pangs
Some borne on stretchers dreamed of home,
Dear things, war-blotted from their hearts.

A man's brains splattered on
A stretcher-bearer's face;
His shook shoulders slipped their load,
But when they bent to look again
The drowning soul was sunk too deep
For human tenderness.

They left this dead with the older dead,
Stretched at the cross roads.
Burnt black by strange decay,
Their sinister faces lie
The lid over each eye,
The grass and coloured clay

More motion have than they,
Joined to the great sunk silences.

Here is one not long dead;
His dark hearing caught our far wheels,
And the choked soul stretched weak hands
To reach the living word the far wheels said,
The blood-dazed intelligence beating for light,
Crying through the suspense of the far torturing wheels
Swift for the end to break,
Or the wheels to break,
Cried as the tide of the world broke over his sight.

Will they come? Will they ever come?
Even as the mixed hoofs of the mules,
The quivering-bellied mules,
And the rushing wheels all mixed
With his tortured upturned sight,
So we crashed round the bend,
We heard his weak scream,
We heard his very last sound,
And our wheels grazed his dead face.

                                                    1917

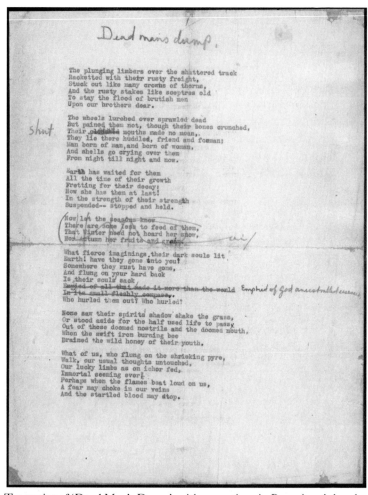

The plunging limbers over the shattered track
Racketted with their rusty freight,
Stuck out like many crowns of thorns,
And the rusty stakes like sceptres old
To stay the flood of brutish men
Upon our brothers dear.

The wheels lurched over sprawled dead
But pained them not, though their bones crunched,
Their shut mouths made no moan,
They lie there huddled, friend and foeman,
Man born of man, and born of woman,
And shells go crying over them
From night till night and now.

Earth has waited for them
All the time of their growth
Fretting for their decay:
Now she has them at last!
In the strength of their strength
Suspended-- stopped and held.

Now let the seasons know
There are some less to feed of them,
That Winter need not hoard her snow,
Nor Autumn her fruits and grain.

What fierce imaginings their dark souls lit
Earth! have they gone into you?
Somewhere they must have gone,
And flung on your hard back
Is their souls' sack,
Emptied of God ancestralled essences,
Who hurled them out? Who hurled?

None saw their spirits shadow shake the grass,
Or stood aside for the half used life to pass
Out of those doomed nostrils and the doomed mouth,
When the swift iron burning bee
Drained the wild honey of their youth.

What of us, who flung on the shrieking pyre,
Walk, our usual thoughts untouched,
Our lucky limbs as on ichor fed,
Immortal seeming ever?
Perhaps when the flames beat loud on us,
A fear may choke in our veins
And the startled blood may stop.

Typescript of 'Dead Man's Dump', with corrections in Rosenberg's hand
(Imperial War Museum).

The air is loud with death,
The dark air spurts with fire
The explosions ceaseless are,
Timelessly now, some minutes past,
These dead strode time with vigorous life,
Till the shrapnel called 'an end!'
But not to all. In bleeding pangs,
Some born on stretchers, dreamed of home,
Dear things, war-blotted from their hearts.

A man's brains splattered on
A stretcher bearer's face;
His shook shoulders slipped its load,
But when they bent to look again,
The drowning soul was sunk too deep
For human tenderness.

They left this dead with the older dead,
Stretched at the cross roads.

Burnt black by strange decay,
Their sinister faces lie
The lid over each eye,
The grass and coloured clay
More motion have than they,
Joined to the great sunk silences.

Here is one not long dead;
His dark hearing caught our far wheels,
And the choked soul stretched weak hands
To reach the living word the far wheels said,
The blood dazed intelligence beating for light,
Crying through the suspense of the far torturing wheels,
Swift for the end to break,
Or the wheels to break,
Cried as the tide of the world broke over his sight.

Will they come? Will they ever come?
Even as the mixed hoofs of the mules,
The quivering bellied mules,
And the rushing wheels all mixed
With his tortured upturned sight,
So we crashed round the bend,
We heard his weak scream,
We heard his very last sound,
And our wheels grazed his dead face.

Isaac Rosenberg
May 14. 1917
B.E.F. France

105

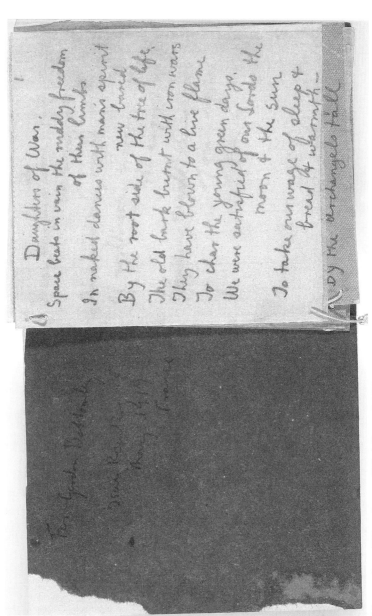

Manuscript of 'Daughters of War' (Imperial War Museum).

DAUGHTERS OF WAR

Space beats the ruddy freedom of their limbs –
Their naked dances with man's spirit naked
By the root side of the tree of life,
(The underside of things
And shut from earth's profoundest eyes).

I saw in prophetic gleams
These mighty daughters in their dances
Beckon each soul aghast from its crimson corpse
To mix in their glittering dances.
I heard the mighty daughters' giant sighs
In sleepless passion for the sons of valour,
And envy of the days of flesh
Barring their love with mortal boughs across –
The mortal boughs – the mortal tree of life.
The old bark burnt with iron wars
They blow to a live flame
To char the young green days
And reach the occult soul; they have no softer lure
No softer lure than the savage ways of death.

We were satisfied of our lords the moon and the sun
To take our wage of sleep and bread and warmth –
These maidens came – these strong ever-living Amazons,
And in an easy might their wrists
Of night's sway and noon's sway the sceptres brake,
Clouding the wild – the soft lustres of our eyes.

Clouding the wild lustres, the clinging tender lights;
Driving the darkness into the flame of day,
With the Amazonian wind of them

Over our corroding faces
That must be broken – broken for evermore
So the soul can leap out
Into their huge embraces.
Though there are human faces
Best sculptures of Deity,
And sinews lusted after
By the Archangels tall,
Even these must leap to the love heat of these maidens
From the flame of terrene days
Leaving grey ashes to the wind – to the wind.

One (whose great lifted face,
Where wisdom's strength and beauty's strength
And the thewed strength of large beasts
Moved and merged, gloomed and lit)
Was speaking, surely, as the earth-men's earth fell away;
Whose new hearing drunk the sound
Where pictures, lutes, and mountains mixed
With the loosed spirit of a thought.
Essenced to language, thus –

'My sisters force their males
From the doomed earth, from the doomed glee
And hankering of hearts.
Frail hands gleam up through the human quagmire and lips of ash
Seem to wail, as in sad faded paintings
Far sunken and strange.
My sisters have their males
Clean of the dust of old days
That clings about those white hands
And yearns in those voices sad.

But these shall not see them,
Or think of them in any days or years,
They are my sisters' lovers in other days and years.'

1917

SOLDIER: TWENTIETH CENTURY

I love you, great new Titan!
Am I not you?
Napoleon and Caesar
Out of you grew.

Out of unthinkable torture,
Eyes kissed by death,
Won back to the world again,
Lost and won in a breath,

Cruel men are made immortal.
Out of your pain born.
They have stolen the sun's power
With their feet on your shoulders worn.

Let them shrink from your girth,
That has outgrown the pallid days,
When you slept like Circe's swine,
Or a word in the brain's ways.

                                    1917

GIRL TO SOLDIER ON LEAVE

I love you – Titan lover,
My own storm-days' Titan.
Greater than the son of Zeus,
I know who I would choose.

Titan – my splendid rebel –
The old Prometheus
Wanes like a ghost before your power –
His pangs were joys to yours.

Pallid days arid and wan
Tied your soul fast.
Babel cities' smoky tops
Pressed upon your growth

Weary gyves. What were you,
But a word in the brain's ways,
Or the sleep of Circe's swine?
One gyve holds you yet.

It held you hiddenly on the Somme
Tied from my heart at home.
O must it loosen now? I wish
You were bound with the old old gyves.

Love! you love me – your eyes
Have looked through death at mine.
You have tempted a grave too much.
I let you – I repine.

1917

THE BURNING OF THE TEMPLE

Fierce wrath of Solomon
Where sleepest thou? O see
The fabric which thou won
Earth and ocean to give thee –
O look at the red skies.

Or hath the sun plunged down?
What is this molten gold –
These thundering fires blown
Through heaven – where the smoke rolled?
Again the great king dies.

His dreams go out in smoke,
His days he let not pass
And sculptured here are broke
Are charred as the burnt grass
Gone as his mouth's last sighs.

1918

THE DESTRUCTION OF JERUSALEM BY THE BABYLONIAN HORDES

They left their Babylon bare
Of all its tall men.
Of all its proud horses;
They made for Lebanon.

And shadowy sowers went
Before their spears to sow
The fruit whose taste is ash
For Judah's soul to know.

They who bowed to the Bull god
Whose wings roofed Babylon,
In endless hosts darkened
The bright-heavened Lebanon.

They washed their grime in pools
Where laughing girls forgot
The wiles they used for Solomon.
Sweet laughter! remembered not.

Sweet laughter charred in the flame
That clutched the cloud and earth
While Solomon's towers crashed between
The gird of Babylon's mirth.

1918

'THROUGH THESE PALE COLD DAYS'

Through these pale cold days
What dark faces burn
Out of three thousand years,
And their wild eyes yearn,

While underneath their brows
Like waifs their spirits grope
For the pools of Hebron again –
For Lebanon's summer slope.

They leave these blond still days
In dust behind their tread
They see with living eyes
How long they have been dead.

1918

LETTERS

ABERCROMBIE, Lascelles (1881–1938), poet and critic, was a friend of Edward Marsh and a founder member of the 'Georgian' poetry movement in 1912. One of Rosenberg's most admired mentors, he later became Professor of English Literature first at Leeds University, then at Bedford College, London University.

AMSCHEWITZ, John Henry, R.B.A., professional artist and friend and neighbour of the Rosenberg family. He advised Isaac Rosenberg to go to evening classes at Birkbeck School of Art. At his studio he introduced Rosenberg to fellow artists, and he painted the earliest known portrait of Rosenberg in 1911, which was presented to Jew's College by the Polish-Jewish actor Michael Sherbrooke, whom Rosenberg had met at Amschewitz's studio.

BINYON, Laurence (1869–1943), poet and art critic, worked in the Department of Prints and Drawings at the British Museum, becoming Keeper in 1932. He was Professor of Poetry at Harvard University in 1933–34. Rosenberg wrote to him and was invited to meet him at the British Museum. Binyon helped and encouraged him with his poetry and corresponded with him regularly until Rosenberg's death in 1918. He wrote the Introductory Memoir to the selection of *Poems by Isaac Rosenberg* published in 1922.

BOMBERG, David (1890–1957), artist and close friend of Rosenberg. The son of immigrant Polish Jews, Bomberg was one of the group of talented young men that included Joseph Leftwich, Samuel Winsten, John Rodker, Mark Gertler and Rosenberg, who became known as 'the Whitechapel Boys'. They frequented the Whitechapel Library and Art Gallery, and went on to become writers and artists. Bomberg went to the Slade School of Fine Art with Rosenberg, but became much more committed to radical avant-garde ideas. While still at the Slade in 1913 Bomberg was developing Cubist techniques and became a founder member of the London Group. He was also invited to exhibit at the Vorticist Exhibition of 1915. He enlisted with the Royal Engineers in 1915, and after the war travelled widely, while his work became centred on landscape. Out of fashion in the inter-war years, he eventually became an influential teacher of art at the Borough Polytechnic in South London, founding the Borough Group.

BOTTOMLEY, Gordon (1874–1948), professional poet and dramatist of the 'Georgian' movement. Although they never met, Rosenberg much admired his work, and from June 1916 Bottomley encouraged and corresponded with him, reading and commenting on his poems until Rosenberg's death in 1918. Bottomley and his literary executors ensured the survival of many of Rosenberg's original manuscripts and drawings. Bottomley selected and edited the first posthumous collection of Rosenberg's work, *Poems by Isaac Rosenberg* (1922) and collaborated with the critic D.W. Harding on the *Collected Works* (1937).

GERTLER, Mark (1891-1939), artist and one of the 'Whitechapel Boys'. The son of Polish-Jewish immigrants in Stepney, Gertler attended the Slade School of Fine Art from 1908, overlapping with Bomberg and Rosenberg. He recommended the Post-Impressionists to Rosenberg, and introduced him to Edward Marsh at the Café Royal in November 1913. A member of the London Group and the New English Art Club, he became a conscientious objector during the war, and was taken up by Lady Ottoline Morrell and her circle. He had a famously unhappy love affair with fellow Slade artist Dora Carrington. Gertler's work, like Bomberg's, fell out of fashion after the war and he committed suicide in 1939.

JOSEPH, Mrs Lily Delissa, wealthy Jewish patron of Rosenberg. She met Rosenberg while he was copying in the National Gallery and engaged him as her son's art tutor. She was the sister of the artist

Solomon J. Solomon R.A. and of Mrs Henrietta Löwy. These two sisters (together with a third lady, Mrs Herbert Cohen) clubbed together to send Rosenberg to the Slade School of Fine Art.

LOWY, Ruth, the daughter of Mrs Henrietta Löwy. She became a fellow student of Rosenberg's at the Slade School of Fine Art, discussed painting with him and modelled for him. She later married the publisher Victor Gollancz.

MARSH, Edward (later Sir Edward) (1872–1955), patron of the arts and career civil servant, private secretary to Winston Churchill during the First World War. The compiler of five successful volumes of *Georgian Poetry* from 1912 to 1922 and a discerning collector of contemporary works of art, Marsh devoted his small private income to supporting young artists and writers, including many of the 'Whitechapel Boys'. He was Rosenberg's most important and long-standing patron, buying his paintings, including *Sacred Love*, and published an extract from 'Moses' in *Georgian Poetry 1916–17*. Marsh read and criticized Rosenberg's poems and corresponded with him faithfully until Rosenberg's death in 1918. Rosenberg's last letter and poem were sent to Marsh the day before he died.

RODKER, John (1894–1955), author, translator, poet and publisher, and one of the 'Whitechapel Boys'. The son of an East End Jewish corset-maker, Rodker wrote poems and kept in touch with Rosenberg until Rosenberg's death in 1918. Rosenberg painted Rodker's portrait and that of his wife Sonia. Like Rosenberg's other childhood friend, the poet Samuel Winsten, Rodker was imprisoned for being a conscientious objector during the war. He promoted Rosenberg's work to his contacts and sent Rosenberg's poem 'Marching' to *Poetry* (Chicago) in January 1916. In his final years Rodker ran a successful small publishing business, the Imago Press.

SCHIFF, Sydney, Jewish writer and translator under the pen name Stephen Hudson. Rosenberg met him in spring 1915, and Schiff corresponded with Rosenberg, reading and commenting on his poems, helping him with gifts of money and artist's materials, and sending him newspapers and books once Rosenberg was sent on active service to France.

SEATON, Winifreda, a middle-aged schoolmistress whom Rosenberg met sometime during 1910 in Amschewitz's studio. She encouraged Rosenberg by reading his poems and lending him books to read, introducing him in particular to Donne and the Metaphysical poets. Rosenberg corresponded with her and continued to send her his poems until his death in 1918.

TREVELYAN, R. C. ('Bob') (1872–1951), prolific poet and translator from Greek and Latin authors. From June 1916 he was a correspondent and supporter of Rosenberg's.

WRIGHT, Alice, a teacher of painting at Birkbeck School of Art. She took Rosenberg for one of his evening classes there from 1908. She continued to help and advise him on his painting when he went to the Slade, and she and her sister also took an active interest in his poetry, introducing him to the work of Blake and Shelley, who profoundly influenced his own work.

To Israel Zangwill

[1910?]   159 Oxford Street,
                                       Mile End, E.

I hope I am not taking too great a presumption by intruding in this matter on your valuable time. If the poems do not merit any part of the time you may do me the honour to bestow on them, then the presumption is the more unpardonable; but though I myself am diffident about them, one has, I suppose, whether one has reason or not, a sort of half-faith; and it is this half-faith – misplaced or not – that has led me to this course. If you think them worth criticism, (which is more than I expect,) on that depends whether this half-faith is to be made an entire one or none at all. I don't know whether it's justifiable, and I do not mention it to abate one jot of your candour, but only in extenuation of my presumption, to remind you that this is not the first time I have wearied you with my specimens of desperate attempts to murder and mutilate King's English beyond all shape of recognition; for about five years ago, when I had just been apprenticed to Carl Hentschel's as a Photo Etcher, I had the hardihood to send you some verses which you were kind enough to think were 'promising', and told me I would hear from you again. Of course, it isn't likely you will remember the occasion, amid your multifarious duties of your valuable life but to me it was an event; and I only mention it to show that I have some sort of right to bother you with these; it being in a way your own kind criticism of the poem five years ago that encouraged me to continue in these,

                        Yours humbly,

                                            ISAAC ROSENBERG

Extracts from letters to Miss Seaton [before 1911]

It is horrible to think that all these hours, when my days are full of vigour and my hands and soul craving for self-expression, I am bound, chained to this fiendish mangling-machine, without hope and almost desire of deliverance, and the days of youth go by . . . I have tried to make some sort of self-adjustment to circumstances by saying, 'It is all *experience*'; but, good God! it is *all* experience, and nothing else . . . I really would like to take up painting seriously; I think I might do something at that; but poetry – I despair of ever writing excellent poetry. I can't look at things in the simple, large way that great poets do. My mind is so cramped and dulled and fevered, there is no consistency of purpose, no oneness of aim; the very fibres are torn apart, and application deadened by the fiendish persistence of the coil of circumstance.

[*1911*]

Congratulate me! I've cleared out of the – shop, I hope for good and all. I'm free – free to do anything, hang myself or anything except work . . . I'm very optimistic, now that I don't know what to do, and everything seems topsy-turvy.

*   *   *

I am out of work. I doubt if I feel the better for it, much as the work was distasteful, though I expect it's the hankering thought of the consequences, pecuniary, etc., that bothers me . . . All one's thoughts seem to revolve round to one point – death. It is horrible, especially at night, 'in the silence of the midnight'; it seems to clutch at your thought – you can't breathe. Oh, I think, work, work, any work, only to stop one thinking.

*   *   *

One conceives one's lot (I suppose it's the same with all people, no matter what their condition) to be terribly tragic. You are the victim of a horrible conspiracy; everything is unfair. The gods have either forgotten you or made you a sort of scapegoat to bear all the punishment. I believe, however hard one's lot is, one ought to try and accommodate oneself to the conditions; and except in a case of purely physical pain, I think it can be done. Why not make the very utmost of our lives? . . . I'm a practical economist in this respect. I endeavour to waste nothing . . . Waste words! Not to talk is to waste words . . .

To most people life is a musical instrument on which they are unable to play: but in the musician's hands it becomes a living thing . . . The artist can see beauty everywhere, anywhere . . .

*   *   *

You mustn't forget the circumstances I have been brought up in, the little education I have had. Nobody ever told me what to read, or ever put poetry in my way. I don't think I knew what real poetry was till I read Keats a couple of years ago. True, I galloped through Byron when I was about fourteen, but I fancy I read him more for the story than for the poetry. I used to try to imitate him. Anyway, if I didn't quite take to Donne at first, you understand why. Poetical appreciation is only newly bursting on me. I always enjoyed Shelley and Keats. The 'Hyperion' ravished me . . .

Whenever I read anything in a great man's life that pulls him down to me, my heart always pleads for him, and my mind pictures extenuating circumstances.

*   *   *

Have you ever picked up a book that looks like a Bible on the outside, but is full of poetry or comic within? My Hood is like that, and, I am afraid, so am I. Whenever I feel inclined to laugh, my visage assumes the longitude and gravity of a church spire.

*   *   *

I can't say I have ever experienced the power of one spirit over another except in books, of course, at least in any intense way that you mean. Unless you mean the interest one awakes in us, and we long to know more, and none other. I suppose we are all influenced by everybody we come in contact with, in a subconscious way, if not direct, and everything that happens to us is experience; but only the few know it. Most people can only see and hear the noisy sunsets, mountains and waterfalls; but the delicate greys and hues, the star in the puddle, the quiet sailing cloud, is nothing to them. Of course, I only mean this metaphorically, as distinguishing between obvious experiences and the almost imperceptible. I still have no work to do. I think, if nothing turns up here, I will go to Africa. I could not

123

endure to live upon my people; and up till now I have been giving them from what I had managed to save up when I was at work. It is nearly run out now, and if I am to do nothing, I would rather do it somewhere else. Besides, I feel so cramped up here, I can do no drawing, reading, or anything . . .

Create our own experience! We can, but we don't. Very often it's only the trouble of a word, and who knows what we miss through not having spoken? It's the man with impudence who has more experience than anybody. He not only varies his own, but makes other people's his own.

*   *   *

Do I like music, and what music I like best? I know nothing whatever about music. Once I heard Schubert's 'Unfinished Symphony' at the band; and – well, I was in heaven. It was a blur of sounds – sweet, fading and blending. It seemed to draw the sky down, the whole spirit out of me; it was articulate feeling. The inexpressible in poetry, in painting, was there expressed. But I have not heard much, and the sensation that gave me I never had again. I should like very much to be one of the initiated.

*   *   *

Some more confidences. I've discovered I'm a very bad talker: I find it difficult to make myself intelligible at times; I can't remember the exact word I want, and I think I leave the impression of being a rambling idiot.

*   *   *

The thoroughness is astounding. No slipshod, tricky slickness, trusting to chance effects, but a subtle suggestiveness, and accident that is the consequence of intention.

Thanks so much for the Donne. I had just been reading Ben Jonson again, and from his poem to Donne he must have thought him a giant. I have read some of the Donne; I have certainly never come across anything so choke-full of profound meaningful ideas. It would have been very difficult for him to express something commonplace, if he had to.

124

I forgot to ask you to return my poetry, as I mean to work on some. I agree the emotions are not worth expressing, but I thought the things had some force, and an idea or so I rather liked. Of course, I know poetry is a far finer thing than that, but I don't think the failure was due to the subject – I had nothing to say about it, that's all. Crashaw, I think, is sometimes very sexual in his religious poems, but it is always new and beautiful. I believe we are apt to fix a standard (of subject) in poetry. We acknowledge the poetry in subjects not generally taken as material, but I think we all (at least I do) prefer the poetical subject – 'Kubla Khan', 'The Mistress of Vision', 'DreamTryst' [by Francis Thompson]; Poe, Verlaine. Here feeling is separated from intellect; our senses are not interfered with by what we know of facts: we know infinity through melody.

*　　　*　　　*

[*Postmarked August 10, 1912*]　　　　　　32 Carlingford Road
Hampstead
Friday

DEAR MISS WRIGHT

I have not seen the pearl by day but it looks gorgeous by night – it is just that iride[sce]nce – that shimmering quality I want to make the whole scheme of my picture – and that will help me tremendously – Thank you so much – I had Miss Grimshaw this afternoon and we both worked hard – She is a very good sitter – though her figure was much too scraggy for my purpose – I practically finished the drapery, and the upper part I will do from some more titanic model if I can get the type –

I forgot when you were here to ask you to put your names in the Shelley you gave me – I think a present is no present without the – I mean a book is no present without it has the names of the giver – I would appreciate it very much – I owe some of the most wonderful sensations I have ever experienced to that book – the speech by Beatrice about death [from *The Cenci*] – I think it is quite

125

the most intense passage in the whole of literature – the literature I
know.

Yours sincerely

ISAAC ROSENBERG

[*Postmarked September 16, 1912*]   159 Oxford St

Mile End E

DEAR MISS WRIGHT

I was far from expecting the pleasure that awaited me when I got
home last night in your letter and your sister's poems. I read them
while having supper, and, I can assure you, I have seldom enjoyed a
supper more, a proof that the ordinary material facts of life can be
made more pleasurable with the assistance of some intellectual
garnish. They seem to me very beautiful, though I cannot quite agree
with the pessimistic tone of the mirror poem. When Milton writes on
his blindness, how dignified he is! how grand, how healthy! What
begins in a mere physical moan, concludes in a grand triumphant spir-
itual expression, of more than resignation, of conquest. But I think
the concluding idea very beautiful. I like the sonnets very much, an
uncommon artistic expression of the artist's common lament. But this
pettifogging, mercantile, money-loving age is deaf, dead as their dead
idol gold, and dead as that to all higher enobling influences.

After seeing these, the poems, I wonder how I could ever have
shown mine; still, you must understand I showed mine not so much
out of vanity, as, on the contrary, out of a consciousness of their
poverty, to have their defects pointed out.

I should be much obliged for a criticism.

Yours,

ISAAC ROSENBERG

To Laurence Binyon [*1912*]

I must thank you very much for your encouraging reply to my
poetical efforts . . . As you are kind enough to ask about myself, I am

sending a sort of autobiography I wrote about a year ago . . . You will see from that that my circumstances have not been very favourable for artistic production; but generally I am optimistic, I suppose because I am young and do not properly realize the difficulties. I am now attending the Slade, being sent there by some wealthy Jews who are kindly interested in me, and, of course, I spend most of my time drawing. I find writing interferes with drawing a good deal, and is far more exhausting.

[*No date. Presumably Oct. 1912*]   32 Carlingford Road
                                                                    Hampstead

DEAR MRS COHEN

I am very sorry I have disappointed you. If you tell me what was expected of me I shall at least have the satisfaction of knowing by how much I have erred. You were disappointed in my picture for its unfinished state – I have no wish to defend myself – or I might ask what you mean by finish: – and you are convinced I could have done better. I thank you for the compliment but I do not think it deserved – I did my best.

You did ask me whether I had been working hard, and I was so taken back at the question that I couldn't think what to say. If you did not think the work done sufficient evidence, what had I to say? I have no idea what you expected to see. I cannot conceive who gave you the idea that I had such big notions of myself, are you sure the people you enquired of know me, and meant me. You say people I have lately come in contact with. I have hardly seen anyone during the holidays – and I certainly have not been ashamed of my opinions, not about myself, but others – when I have; and if one does say anything in an excited unguarded moment – perhaps an expression of what one would like to be – it is distorted and interpreted as conceit – when in honesty it should be overlooked. I am not very inquisitive naturally, but I think it concerns me to know what you mean by poses and mannerisms – and whose advice do I not take who are in a position to give – and what more healthy style of work do you wish me to adopt?

I feel very grateful for your interest in me – going to the Slade

Isaac Rosenberg (extreme left) with fellow students at the Slade School 1912–13, including David Bomberg (back row, third from left), Dora Carrington (front row, extreme left, with stick), C. D. W. Nevinson (front row, wearing braces), Mark Gertler (middle of front row, with stovepipe hat), and Stanley Spencer (front row, second from right).

has shown possibilities – has taught me to see more accurately. – but one especial thing it has shown me – Art is not a plaything, it is blood and tears, it must grow up with one; and I believe I have begun too late.

I suppose I go on as I am till Xmas. Till then I will look about. I should like all the money advanced on me considered as a loan – but which you must not expect back for some years as it takes some time settling down in art.

Yours sincerely

I ROSENBERG

The Slade pictures will be on view shortly, I will let you know more if you care to see them.

DEAR MISS SEATON

Excuse me writing in pencil as my pen has gone wrong and I want to write just now. I have not been reading Donne much as I am drawing a lot, and when I'm not drawing my mind is generally occupied that way. A great deal of Donne seems a sort of mental gymnastics, the strain is very obvious, but he is certainly wonderful, 'The ecstasy' is very fine, but F. Thompson's 'Dream tryst' to me is much finer. There is a small book of contemporary Belgian poetry like the German you lent me (which by the way I don't feel inclined to open) some Maeterlincks seem marvellous to me, and Verhaern [Emile Verhaeren] in the 'Sovran Rythm' knocks Donne into a cocked hat. I mean for genuine poetry, where the words lose their interest as words and only a living and beautiful idea remains. It is a grand conception, – Eve meeting Adam. [Maurice] Maeterlinck has a superb little thing 'Orison' – a most trembling fragile moan of astonishing beauty. The Blakes at the Tate show that England has turned out one man second to none who has ever lived. The drawings are finer than his poems, much clearer, though I can't help thinking it was unfortunate that he did not live when a better tradition of drawing ruled. His conventional manner of expressing those astounding conceptions is the fault of his time, not his.

Yours sincerely

ISAAC ROSENBERG

DEAR MR LESSER

I have failed in the Prix De Rorne competition, but when I get the things back, I can do a little more to them and send them to Exhibitions. Since I did those things I have been unwell, and been coughing very badly for about two months. Last week I saw a doctor and though at first he thought it was serious and said I had a very bad chest, the next time he said it wasn't so bad but I needed to go away for a couple of weeks and be out in the open. I have been sleeping here while unwell. Do you think the Society would let me have some money to go away so that I would be fairly comfortable and I could go somewhere on the South Coast.

The 'Prix De Rome' things, successful and not, are on show at the Imperial Institute, South Kensington, from 10 till 4, all this week. No Slade people got it, though Prof Tonks thought they should have done so. He was disgusted with the decision. I trust you will let me know soon.

Your's [sic] sincerely

ISAAC ROSENBERG

[*1913? December*]   87 Dempsey St
Stepney E

DEAR MARSH

Thanks very very much for the book. I know so little of these men, and from that little[,] I know how much I miss by not knowing more. I think the Queen's song of [James Elroy] Flecker, delicious; and 'The end of the world' by [Gordon] Bottomley, very fine imagination and original. That is all I have had time to read yet. What strikes me about these men [is] they are very much alive, and have personal vision – and what is so essential, can express themselves very simply. But writing about a poem is like singing about a song – or rather, as Donne says, fetching water to the sea, and in my case, very dirty water. You can talk about life, but you can only talk round literature; you will be talking about life, I think.

Yours sincerely

ISAAC ROSENBERG

[*Postcard to his mother,*   195 Wimbourne Rd
postmarked February 24, 1914]   Winton Bournemouth
c/o Cohen

I forgot to put the address yesterday. I'm not lucky with the weather yet but the air is very good, – I don't cough much. The town here is like a big sanatorium. I'll send a card of the invalids' garden. Pine Woods a few minutes from here[.] I'm going there now[.]

ISAAC

[No date, but must be Spring 1914]   87 Dempsey St
                                         Stepney E

DEAR MR LESSER

Do you think the E A S [Jewish Educational Aid Society] would make me a grant of 12 or 15 pounds to go to S. Africa.

The doctor has told me my chest is weak and that I must live in the country and take care of myself. I cannot live here in the country just now, and it is now that it is so essential. I have a relation in Cape Town who could put me up until I sold things some way or other, and I believe I could get heaps of good subject matter.

The kaffirs would sit for practically nothing. In a year I'd have a lot of interesting stuff, to send to England. I am sending several things to Whitechapel show. The fare to S. Africa is £12. Could you let me know at once as I am convinced of the importance of not stopping here.

Your's [*sic*] sincerely

ISAAC ROSENBERG

To Miss Seaton [Spring 1914]

So I've decided on Africa, the climate being very good, and I believe plenty to do . . . I won't be quite lost in Africa . . . I dislike London for the selfishness it instils into one, which is a reason of the peculiar feeling of isolation I believe most people have in London. I hardly know anybody whom I would regret leaving (except, of course, the natural ties of sentiment with one's own people); but whether it is that my nature distrusts people, or is intolerant, or whether my pride or my backwardness cools people, I have always been alone. Forgive this little excursion into the forbidden lands of egotism.

[May–June 1914]   87 Dempsey St
                      Stepney E

DEAR MARSH

This is my rest while packing. My things have to be on board by Wed – and I only knew today – so you can imagine the rush I'm

131

in. Your criticism gave me great pleasure; not so much the criticism, as to feel that you took those few lines up so thoroughly, and tried to get into them. You don[']t know how encouraging that is. People talk about independence and all that – but one always works with some sort of doubt, that is, if one believes in the inspired 'suntreaders'. I believe that all poets who are personal – see things genuinely, have their place. One needn't be a Shakespeare. Yet I never meant to go as high as these – I know I've come across things by people of far inferior vision, that were as important in their results, to me.

I am not going to refute your criticisms; in literature I have no judgment – at least for style. If in reading a thought has expressed itself to me, in beautiful words; my ignorance of grammar etc, makes me accept that. I should think you are right mostly; and I may yet work away your chief objections. You are quite right in the way you read my poem ['Midsummer Frost', see p. 65] but I thought I could use the 'July ghost' to mean the Summer, and also an ambassador of the summer, without interfering with the sense. The shell of thought is man; you realise a shell has an opening. Across this opening, the ardours – the sense of heat forms a web – this signifies a sense of summer – the web again becomes another metaphor – a July ghost. But of course I mean it for summer right through, I think your suggestion of taking out 'woven' is very good. I enclose another thing which is part of this. I told you my idea – The whole thing is to be called the poet, and begins with the way external nature affects him, and goes on to human nature.

In packing my things I found a little painting of a boy that I dont think looks at all bad. I could show it to you if you cared to see it –

Yours sincerely

ISAAC ROSENBERG

43 De Villiers St
C T

[*Letter Card from Capetown,*
postmarked June 20 or 30, 1914]

DEAR MARSH

I've had a fearfully busy week – seeing people and preparing for work. I want to write a long letter I have lots to write about, –

132

wait till next week. [Sir Herbert] Stanley has given me a small job – painting two babies. I'm just off to do them.

The place is gorgeous – just for an artist.

Yours sincerely

ISAAC ROSENBERG

[*Postmarked Capetown, ?July 24, 1914*]   43 Devilliers St
Cape Town

DEAR MARSH

I should like you to do me a favour if it[']s not putting you to too much bother. I am in an infernal city by the sea. This city has men in it – and these men have souls in them – or at least have the passages to souls. Though they are millions of years behind time they have yet reached the stage of evolution that knows ears and eyes. But these passages are dreadfully clogged up; gold dust, diamond dust, stocks and shares, and heaven knows what other flinty muck. Well I've made up my mind to clear through all this rubbish. But I want your help. Now I'm going to give a series of lectures on modern art (I'm sending you the first, which I gave in great style. I was asked whether the futurist[s] exhibited at the Royal Academy.) But I want to make the lectures interesting and intelligible by reproductions or slides. Now I wonder whether you have reproductions which you could lend me till I returned or was finished with them. I want to talk about [Augustus] John, Cézanne, Van Gogh, [J. D.] Innes, the early Picasso (not the cubist one), [Stanley] Spencer, [Mark] Gertler, [Henry] Lamb. Puvis De Chavannes, Degas. A book of reproductions of the P Impressionist[s] would do and I could get them transferred on slides. I hope this would not put you to any great trouble but if you could manage to do it you dont know how you would help me. Epstien [*sic*: Jacob Epstein] . . .

Stanley gave me a little job to paint two babies, which helped me to pay my way for a bit. I expect to get pupils and kick up a row with my lectures. But nobody seems to have money here, and not an ounce of interest in Art. The climate's fine, but the Sun is a very changeable creature and I can't come to any sort of understanding with this golden beast. He pretends to keep quiet for half an hour and just as I think, now I've got it, the damnid [*sic*] thing has frisked about.

There's a lot of splended stuff to paint. We are walled in by the sharp upright mountain and the bay. Across the bay the piled up mountains of Africa look lovely and dangerous. It makes one think of savagery and earthquakes – the elemental lawlessness. You are lucky to be in comfortable London and its armchair culture.

I've painted a Kaffir, and am pottering about. I expect if I get pupils to get a room and shall be able to work better. Do write to me – think of me, a creature of the most exquisite civilization, planted in this barbarous land. Write me of Spencer, Lamb, Currie and the pack of them. I mean to write to Gertler myself, but so far I've not been able to get away from my own people here to write. They don't understand the artist's seclusion to concentrate, and I'm always interrupted. Write me of poetry and do send me that little thing of Binyon's in your album.

Yours sincerely

Isaac Rosenberg

I'll send my lecture next week as they may be printing it in a local paper.

[Postmarked Capetown, August 8, 1914]   'Hill House'
43 Devilliers St
Cape Town

Dear Marsh

I enclose the lecture. By the time it reaches you I expect the world will be in convulsions and you'll be in the thick of it. I know my poor innocent essay stands no chance by the side of the bristling legions of warscented documents on your desk; but know that I despise war and hate war, and hope that the Kaiser William will have his bottom smacked – a naughty aggressive schoolboy who will have *all* the plum pudding. Are we going to have Tennyson's 'Battle in the air', and the nations deluging the nations with blood from the air? Now is the time to go on an exploring expedition to the North Pole; to come back and find settled order again.

Yours sincerely

Isaac Rosenberg

'Hill House'
                                                                43 de Villiers St
                                                                Cape Town

DEAR MARSH

You are very kind to think of me. I see though from the papers your friend is not coming out but is going to hotter places than this. It[']s a fearful nuisance, this war. 1 think the safest place is at the front, – we'll starve or die of suspense, anywhere else.

I feel very much better in health; I keep a good deal in the open and walk a[?]lot]. We have had very damp weather and wonderful storms and winds; houses blown over, – the very mountains shaken. We are expecting the fine weather, which I mean to see right through and then come back. I've been trying to get pupils to teach, but this war has killed all that. I painted a very interesting girl, which I'm rather pleased with. It's very quiet and modest and no fireworks. I may send it to the New English if I don't bring it back myself in time. Also a self portrait, very gay and cocky, which I think will go down very well. I'm waiting for better weather to paint the kaffirs against characteristic landscapes. Also I've written poems, of which I'm sending the small ones. By the time you get this things will only have just begun I'm afraid; Europe will have just stepped into its bath of blood. I will be waiting with beautiful drying towels of painted canvas, and precious ointments to smear and heal the soul; and lovely music and poems. But I really hope to have a nice lot of pictures and poems by the time all is settled again; and Europe is repenting of her savageries.

I know Duncan Grant's dance and if the one you have is better, it must be very fine indeed. I've just written to Cokeham [Stanley Spencer, known as 'Cookham']; I hadn't his address so sent it to Cokeham on Thames. I hope he got it. His brother is very lucky. I also just wrote to Gertler. I really get no privacy here and can't write or even think. But this coming away has changed me marvellously, and makes me more confident and mature. Here's a chance to exercise any bloodthirsty and critical propensities.

['The Female God', *see p. 58*]

This is the last thing I've written but I've got more, which I may enclose in this letter. What's become of [John] Currie?

Yours sincerely

ISAAC ROSENBERG

Berg Collection

[Spring 1915]

87 Dempsey St
Stepney E

DEAR MARSH

I will bring the picture tomorrow. I think you will like to see it, though if I had a little longer on it it would have been very fine indeed but the model cleared off before I could absolutely finish. I've also been working hard at my poems. I'm glad you haven't shown A. my things. I've made that poem quite clear now I think. I've a scheme for a little book called 'Youth', in three parts.

1. Faith and fear.
2. The cynic's lamp.
3. Sunfire.

In the first the idealistic youth believes and aspires towards purity. The poems are: Aspiration. Song of Immortality (which by the way, is absolutely [Lascelles] Abercrombie's idea in the Hymn to Love, and it[']s one of my first poems). Noon in the city. None know the Lord of the House. A girl's thoughts. Wedded. Midsummer frost.

In the second, The cynic's lamp, the youth has become hardened by bitter experience and has no more vague aspirations, he is just sense. The poems are: Love and lust. In Piccadilly. A mood. The cynic's path. Tess.

In the third, Change and sunfire, the spiritualizing takes place. He has no more illusions, but life itself becomes transfigured through Imagination, that is, real intimacy – love.

The poems are: April dawn. If I am fire. Break in by nearer ways. God made blind etc. Do you like the scheme?

Yours sincerely

ISAAC ROSENBERG

87 Dempsey St
                                                    Stepney E

DEAR MARSH
    Don't you think this is a nice little thing now

The one lost

I mingle with your bones.
You steal in subtle noose
This starry trust He loans,
And in your life I lose.

What will the Lender say
When I shall not be found,
Sought at the Judgement Day,
Lost – in your being bound?

    I've given my things to the printer [the pamphlet *Youth*] – he's
doing 16 pages for £2. 10. I know for certain I can get rid of ten. My
notion in getting them printed is that I believe some of them are
worth reading, and that like money kept from circulating, they
would be useless to myself and others, kept to myself. I lose nothing
by printing and may even make a little money. If you like you can
have my three life drawings for the money if you think they're worth
it. You don't know how happy you have made me by giving me this
chance to print.
                    Yours sincerely
                                            ISAAC ROSENBERG

[Apparently unfinished letter to Ezra Pound, 1915]
87 Dempsey St
Stepney E

DEAR MR POUND

Thank you very much for sending my things to America. As to your suggestion about the army I think the world has been terribly damaged by certain poets (in fact any poet) being sacrificed in this stupid business. There is certainly a strong temptation to join when you are making no money.

[April–May 1915] 87 Dempsey St
Stepney E

DEAR MARSH

I am very sorry to have had to disturb you at such a time with pictures. But when one's only choice is between horrible things you choose the least horrible. First I think of enlisting and trying to get my head blown off, then of getting some manual labour to do – anything – but it seems I'm not fit for anything. Then I took these things to you. You would forgive me if you knew how wretched I was. I am sorry I can give you no more comfort in your own trial but I am going through it too.

Thank you for your cheque[;] it will do for paints and I will try and do something you'll like.

Yours sincerely

ISAAC ROSENBERG

[April–May 1915] 87 Dempsey St
Stepney E

MY DEAR MARSH

Forgive my weak and selfish letter. I should not have disturbed you at all [Rupert Brooke had died on 23 April 1915] but one gets so bewildered in this terrible struggle. Thank you for showing my things to Abercrombie and thinking of that now. He has not written yet. I can come if you like Tuesday or any day. I will come Tue if you do not write.

Yours sincerely

ISAAC ROSENBERG

[June 4th, 1915]   87 Dempsey Street
                                                        Stepney E

DEAR MR SCHIFF

Here are some poems I've had printed [*Youth*]. I am selling them at half [a] crown a book. I am also enclosing a sketch for a play [*Moses*], which may interest you; but I want this back as I have no spare copies.

Hope you enjoyed your holiday. We just missed being blown to pieces by a bomb the other night, a factory near by was burnt to pieces and some people killed.

Yours sincerely

ISAAC ROSENBERG

You will notice I've torn out a page in the book. The poems were very trivial and I've improved the book by taking them out.

[October 1915]   87 Dempsey Street
                                                        Stepney E

DEAR MR SCHIFF

In my last letter I wrote you I was learning 'an honest trade'. I don't know whether I told you what it was but what I meant was that I was learning to do work that I would not be put to all sorts of shifts and diplomatics to dispose of. It is very mechanical work though my skill in drawing is of great use in it. It is process work – preparing blocks for the press – but it is very unhealthy having to be bending over strong acids all day – and though my chest is weak I shall have to forget all that. But I have yet to learn it and when I have learnt it it may take some time before I find work. I am attending an evening school where this work is taught and it may take some months to learn as the hours at the school are so few. I also have to pay this evening school, it is not very much but it is more than I can afford. You have shown that you are interested in me so I thought you would not mind lending me the 10 shillings to pay as it is so very little and I could so easily return it as soon as I get work. I hope you will not think this impudence, but all my friends seem to have disappeared. I hope very soon and by this means that I shall need none.

I am sending some small poems I have managed to write in my awful state of mind, or rather as a relief from it.

Yours sincerely

Isaac Rosenberg

[*October 1915*]   87 Dempsey St
                                                                Stepney E

Dear Mr Schiff

Thank you for the cheque which is as much to me now as all the money in America would be to the Allies. When I am settled I hope you will allow me to return it either in drawings or money. I expect to know enough for my purpose in 2 months, and I will let you know how I get on. As to what you say about my being luckier than other victims I can only say that one's individual situation is more real and important to oneself than the devastation of fates [states] and empires especially when they do not vitally affect oneself. I can only give my personal and if you like selfish point of view that I[,] feeling myself in the prime and vigour of my powers (whatever they may be) have no more free will than a tree; seeing with helpless clear eyes the utter destruction of the railways and avenues of approaches to outer communication cut off. Being by the nature of my upbringing, all my energies having been directed to one channel of activity, crippled from other activities and made helpless even to live. It is true I have not been killed or crippled, been a loser in the stocks, or had to forswear my fatherland, but I have not quite gone free and have a right to say something.

Forgive all this bluster but – salts for constipation – moral of course.

Yours sincerely

Isaac Rosenberg

I have not seen or heard of Bomberg for ages but he was pretty bad 5 months ago.

On Y.M.C.A. notepaper, headed 'H.M. Forces on Active Service'

[*October 1915*]   Priv. I. Rosenberg
                                       Bat. Bantam, Regt. 12th Suffolk,
                                   New Depot, Bury St. Edmunds

DEAR MR SCHIFF,

I could not get the work I thought I might so I have joined this Bantam Battalion (as I was too short for any other) which seems to be the most rascally affair in the world. I have to eat out of a basin together with some horribly smelling scavenger who spits and sneezes into it etc. It is most revolting, at least up to now – I don't mind the hard sleeping the stiff marches etc but this is unbearable. Besides my being a Jew makes it bad amongst these wretches. I am looking forward to having a bad time altogether. I am sending some old things to the New English and if they get in you may see them there. I may be stationed here some time or be drafted off somewhere else; if you write I will be glad to hear[.]

                 Yours sincerely

                                   I. ROSENBERG

[*October 1915*]   12th Suffolks
                                       Bantam Bat.
                               New Offices Recruiting Depot
                                       Bury St Edmunds

DEAR MARSH

I have just joined the Bantams and am down here amongst a horrible rabble – Falstaff's scarecrows were nothing to these. Three out of every 4 have been scavengers[,] the fourth is a ticket of leave. But that is nothing – though while I'm waiting for my kit I'm roughing it a bit having come down without even a towel. I dry my self with my pocket handkerchief. I don't know whether I will be shifted as soon as I get my rigout – I thought you might like to hear this. I meant to send you some poems I wrote which are better than my usual things but I have left them at home where I am rather

141

afraid to go for a while – I left without saying anything. Abercrombie did not write to me, I hope it is not because he disliked my things. If that is not the reason I should like to send him my new things. Can you tell me anything of Gertler.

Yours sincerely

ISAAC ROSENBERG

[*October 1915*]

22648
C Company, 12th Suffolk Bantams
Bury St Edmunds

DEAR MR SCHIFF

You are very good to send me that note. Money is very handy and we get too little of it here. Half of what I get goes to my mother. When I spoke to you of leave I don't think I mentioned that I did not tell my mother I had joined and disappeared without saying anything. It nearly killed my mother I heard[,] and ever since she has been very anxious to see me. I send you here a photo which I think is pretty alive.

What you say about your nephews I dare say is just, but I have been used to this sort of thing and know the kind of people I am with well. I should have been told to soften my boots and I would not have had this damned bother. I now find everybody softens their boots first and anybody would be crippled by wearing them as I have done. I shall let you know when I am in London.

Yours sincerely

ISAAC ROSENBERG

[*November 1915*]

Priv. I. Rosenberg
12th Suffolk Bantams
Military Hospital, Depot, Bury St Edmunds
Tuesday night

DEAR MR SCHIFF

I am still in the hospital and expect to be for at least two days more, so though I have your present for which many thanks, I am unable to make any use of it, but it won't be long before I will be unable to make any more use of it, as it will be used. Just now I don't quite know where I can keep books. I have with me Donne's poems and Brown[e]'s 'Religion De Medici' [*sic*] and must carry both in my pocket. I have drawn some of the chaps in the hospital and I can see heaps of subject matter all over. If you could send any small books or news that might interest me I think I could find a place for them. A small box of watercolours would be handy. I cannot get one in this town. I can only get Sundays off so have no chance of finding out as the evenings are pitch black and no shops are visible. Cigarettes or any small eatable luxuries also help to make things pleasanter. Any sketches I may do I will send though I don't think I'll be in the frame of mind for doing decent work for some time. The only thing (and it is very serious to me) that troubles me is my mother is so upset about me. It was this thought that stopped me from joining long ago.

I hope you are happy with your work. Any kind of work if one [can] only be doing something is what one wants now. I feel very grateful at your appreciation of my position, it keeps the clockwork going. To me this is not a result but one motion of the intricate series of activities that all combine to make a result. One might succumb[,] be destroyed – but one might also (and the chances are even greater for it) be renewed, made larger, healthier. It is not very easy for me to write here as you can imagine and you must not expect any proper continuity or even coherence. But I thought you might like to hear how I am placed exactly and write as I can. If I could get a very small watercolour box with a decent sketch block, pencil, paper about 12 × 10, I might do something Sundays. The landscape is quite good. Hospital incidents are good but I may not be here more than two days. If you could send anything at once I'd get it here. They'd give it me if I had left. With cigarettes I could make myself more liked, and eatables I'd like myself. Cakes chocolates etc. I hope you don't mind this but though they would do this for me at home I don't like my mother to feel I haven't everything I want.

Yours sincerely

I Rosenberg

12th Suffolk Bantams
Military Hospital
Depot
Bury St Edmunds
Sat night

MY DEAR MARSH

I have only just got your letter. They kept it back or it got mislaid – anyway it only reached me today. First not to alarm you by this heading I must tell you that while running before the colonel I started rather excitedly and tripped myself coming down pretty heavily in the wet grit and am in the hospital with both my hands cut. I've been here since last Sat and expect to be out by about the beginning of the week. It is a nondescript kind of life in the hospital and I'm very anxious to get out and be doing some rough kind of work. Mr. Schiff, sent me some watercolours and I amuse myself with drawing the other invalids. Of course I must give them what I do but I can see heaps of material for pictures here. The landscape too seems decent though I haven't seen anything but the Barracks as this accident happened pretty near at the start.

I hope you were not annoyed at that fib of mine but I never dreamt they would trouble to find out at home. I have managed to persuade my mother that I am for home service only, though of course I have signed on for general service. I left without saying anything because I was afraid it would kill my mother or I would be too weak and not go. She seems to have got over it though and as soon as I can get leave I'll see her and I hope it will be well. It is very hard to write here so you must not expect interesting letters [though] there is always behind or through my object some pressing sense of foreign matter, immediate and not personal which hinders and disjoints what would otherwise have coherence and perhaps weight. I have left all my poems including a short drama with a friend and I will write to him for them when I shall send them either direct to Abercrombie or to you first. I believe in myself more as a poet than a painter. I think I get more depth into my writing. I have only taken Donne with me and don't feel for poetry much in this wretched place. There is not a book or paper here, we are not allowed to stir from the gate, have little to eat, and are not allowed to buy any if we have money – and are utterly wretched (I mean the hospital). If you could send me some novel or chocolates, you would make me very happy. I think I will be here (in the hospital) till Tuesday night as it is Sunday tomorrow, and if the doctor says Monday I can leave the hospital, it means Tuesday night. You will get this Mon and I will have a whole day left me to eat a box of chocolates in; it is only a short winter[']s day.

Yours sincerely

Isaac Rosenberg

[*October–November 1915*]   22648
C Company Bantam Bat.
12th Suffolk, Bury St. Edmund[s]

My Dear Marsh

I suppose my troubles are really laughable, but they do irritate at the moment. Doing coal fatigues and cookhouse work with a torn hand and marching ten miles with a clean hole about an inch round in your heel and bullies swearing at you is not very natural. I think when my hands and feet get better I'll enjoy it. Nobody thinks of helping you – I mean those who could. Not till I have been made a thorough cripple[.] An officer said it was absurd to think of wearing those boots and told me to soak it thoroughly in oil to soften it. Thank you for your note, we get little enough you know, and I allow half of that to my mother (I rather fancy she is going to be swindled in this [?] rat trap affair) so it will do to get to London with. You must now be the busiest man in England and I am sure would hardly have time to read my things, besides you won't like the formlessness of the play [*Moses*]. If you like you can send them to Abercrombie and read them when you have more time. I don't think I told you what he said, 'A good many of your poems strike me as experimental and not quite certain of themselves. But on the other hand I always find a vivid and original impulse; and what I like most in your songs is your ability to make the concealed poetic power in words come flashing out. Some of your phrases are remarkable; no one who tries to write poetry would help envying some of them.' I have asked him to sit for me – a poet to paint a poet. All this must seem to you like

145

a blur on the window, or hearing sounds without listening while you are thinking. One blur more and I'll leave you a clean window – I think we're shifting to Shoreham in a week.

Yours sincerely,

Isaac Rosenberg

[*Early December 1915*]

22648

Company C, Bat. Bantam,
Regt. 12th Suffolks, Bury St Edmunds

Dear Mr Schiff

I have a spare moment and am using it to write to you. I feel very bucked this week and as you are interested in my poems I think it will please you too. A letter reached me from Lascelles Abercrombie who I think is our best living poet – this is what he says. 'A good many of your poems strike me as experimental and not quite certain of themselves. But on the other hand I always find a vivid and original impulse; and what I like most in your songs is your ability to make the concealed poetic power in words come flashing out. Some of your phrases are remarkable; no one who writes poetry would help envying some of them.' You must excuse these blots [—] I'm writing from pandemonium and with a rotten pen. I felt A. would sympathise with my work. I haven't been able to draw – we get no private time. The money you sent me I was forced to buy boots with as the military boots rubbed all the skin off my feet and I've been marching in terrible agony. The kind of life does not bother me much. I sleep soundly on boards in the cold; the drills I find fairly interesting, but up till now these accidents have bothered me and I am still suffering with them. My hands are not better and my feet are hell. We have pups for officers – at least one – who seems to dislike me – and you know his position gives him power to make me feel it without me being able to resist. When my feet and hands are better I will slip into the work but as I am it is awkward. The doctor here too, Major Devoral, is a ridiculous bullying brute and I have marked him for special treatment when I come to write about the army. The commanding officer is Major Ogilvie and his adjutant Captain Thornhill. If you happen to know them, all I would want is leave for a weekend to see my mother. I have

146

asked and was told if I got it now I should have none Xmas so I have
put it off. I think we go to Shoreham next week.

Yours sincerely

ISAAC ROSENBERG

I believe I have some pictures in the N.E. but I fancy they are cat-
alogued as Bomberg's but I'm not sure.

[*December 1915*]

Pte I Rosenberg
No 22648
Platoon No 3
12th Suffolks. Hut No 2
Depot. Bury St Edmunds

MY DEAR MARSH

I have devoured your chocolates with the help of some com-
rades and am now out of the hospital. I have been kept very busy
and I find that the actual duties though they are difficult at first and
require all one's sticking power are not in themselves unpleasant, it
is the brutal militaristic bullying meanness of the way they're served
out to us. You're always being threatened with 'clink'. I am sending
you my little play and some poems. The play I mean to work at
when I get a chance. I also enclose a photograph of one of my S
African drawings. When you have read the poems will you send
them to Abercrombie[,] that is if you think he won't be annoyed.

Yours sincerely

I ROSENBERG

Who is the author of Erebus. I have a marvellous poem by him.

[*Late December 1915*]

22648
C Company
12th Suffolk Bantams
Bury St Edmunds

MY DEAR MARSH

I have sent on the poems to L.A. I sent this one as well which I
like ['Marching (As Seen from the Left File)', see p. 78]. But it is

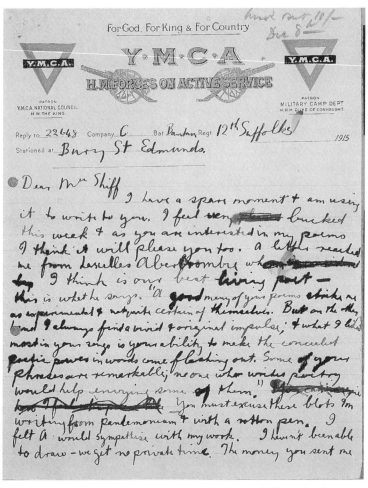

Y·M·C·A

Y.M.C.A.   Y.M.C.A.

H.M. FORCES ON ACTIVE SERVICE

PATRON
Y.M.C.A. NATIONAL COUNCIL
H.M. THE KING

PATRON
MILITARY CAMP DEPT
H.R.H. DUKE OF CONNAUGHT

Reply to 22648 Company C Bat. Bantam Regt 12th Suffolks 1915
Stationed at Bury St Edmunds.

Dear Mr Shiff

I have a spare moment & am using it to write to you. I feel very ~~~ bucked this week & as you are interested in my poems I think it will please you too. A little reached me from Lascelles Abercrombie wh~~ ~~~ I think is our best living poet — this is what he says. "A good many of your poems strike me as experimental & not quite certain of themselves. But on the other hand I always find a vivid & original impulse; & what I like most in your songs is your ability to make the concealed poetic power in words come flashing out. Some of your phrases are remarkable; no one who writes poetry would help envying some of them." ~~~ ~~~ ~~~ ~~~ You must excuse these blots I'm writing from pandemonium & with a rotten pen. I felt you would sympathise with my work. I haven't been able to draw — we get no private time. The money you sent me

Two-page letter on Y.M.C.A. notepaper to Sydney Schiff, no date but early December 1915 (Imperial War Museum).

I was forced to buy boots with as the military boots rubbed all the skin off my feet & I've been marching in terrible agony. The kind of life does not bother me much. I sleep soundly on boards in the cold; the drills I find fairly interesting, but up till now these accidents have bothered me & I am still suffering with them. My hands are not better & my feet are hell. We have pups for officers — at least one — who seems to dislike me — & you know his position gives him power to make me feel it without me being able to resist. When my feet & hands are better I will slip into the work but as I am it is awkward. The doctor here too, Major Devoral, is a ridiculous bullying brute, & I have marked him for special treatment when I come to write about the army. The commanding officer is Major Ogilvie & his adjutant Captain Thornhill. If you happen to know them, all I would want is leave for weekend to see my mother. I have asked & was told if I got it now I should have none Xmas so I have put it off. I think we go to Shoreham next week.

Yours Sincerely
Isaac Rosenberg

I believe I have some pictures in the N.E but I fancy they are catalogued as Bombergs but I'm not sure.

something else I want to write about. I never joined the army from patriotic reasons. Nothing can justify war. I suppose we must all fight to get the trouble over. Anyhow before the war I helped at home when I could and I did other things which helped to keep things going. I thought if I'd join there would be the separation allowance for my mother. At Whitehall it was fixed up that 16/6 would be given including the 3/6 a week deducted from my 7/-. It[']s now between 2 and 3 months since I joined; my 3/6 is deducted right enough, but my mother hasn't received a farthing. The paymaster at barracks of course is no use in this matter. I wonder if you know how these things are managed and what I might do.

Yours sincerely

Isaac Rosenberg

[*Postmarked January 5, 1916*]

22648
12th South Lancashires
A Coy. Alma Barracks
Blackdown Camp
Farnborough

My Dear Marsh

I have been transferred to this reg and am here near Aldershot. Thanks for writing to W.O. I believe my people are getting my 6d a day deducted from my 1s, but not the allowance. We get very little food you know and sometimes none, so if one has only 6d (and often for unaccountable reasons it is not even that) you can imagine what it is like. If I had got into a decent reg that might not have mattered, but amongst the most unspeakably filthy wretches, it is pretty suicidal. I am afraid, though, I'm not in a very happy mood – I have a bad cold through sleeping on a damp floor and have been coal fatigueing all day (a most inhuman job). You must be very busy. – It is a great pity this conscription business, besides the hope it will give to the enemy to have brought England to that step.

I am sorry you didn't like that poem; I thought I had hit on something there.

Yours sincerely

Isaac Rosenberg

I have heard it is not difficult to get a commission. Do you know anything about it?

[*1916, ?March*]
24520
A Coy, 12th South Lancs
Alma Bks, Blackdown Camp
Farnborough, Hants

DEAR MR SCHIFF

I have been in this reg about 2 months now and have been kept going all the time. Except that the food is unspeakable, and perhaps luckily, scanty, the rest is pretty tolerable. I have food sent up from home and that keeps me alive, but as for the others, there is talk of mutiny every day. One reg close by did break out and some men got bayoneted. I don't know when we are going out but the talk is very shortly. I have written two small poems ['Spring 1916' and 'Marching (As Seen from the Left File)', see pp. 86 and 78] since I joined and I think they are my strongest work. I sent them to one or two papers as they are war poems and topical but as I expected, they were sent back. I am afraid my public is still in the womb. Naturally this only has the effect of making me very conceited and to think these poems better than anybody else's. Let me know what you think of them as I have no one to show them to here.

Yours sincerely

ISAAC ROSENBERG

To R. C. Trevelyan

[*Last week of May, 1916*]
22311
A Coy
11th (S) Batt. K.O.R.L. Regt.
Blackdown Camp

DEAR SIR

My friend [John] Rodker told me you liked my poems and wanted a copy. I am enclosing one for you and one for Mr Bottomley (who is the most real poet living in England). They will also send you from home copies (one for Bottomley) of some new poems which I've written since I joined. You will excuse the printer[']s errors as I was not able to correct them. We are leaving for overseas this week (Thursday) but if you write soon I expect I'll get the letter; or write to my people for me Miss A. Rosenberg. 87 Dempsey St. Stepney. London. E. but don't say anything of my being away as my people are Tolstoylians and object to my being in khaki. My reason for 'castrating' my book before I sent it was simply that the poems were commonplace and you would not have said: 'You do it like a navvy' but, 'You do it like a bank clerk.' You have made me very pleased by liking my work and telling me B liked them.

If my people send you a copy bound in cloth you won't mind paying for it, I'm sure[,] as I have not paid the printer yet. 3/6 will do.

Yours sincerely

Isaac Rosenberg

[*Probably May 27, 1916*]   [No address]

Dear Marsh

It was a pity I came late that morning but it could not be helped and I was so anxious to rush my printer through with my poems before I left England. Anyway we're off at last, either tomorrow or Mon. (it[']s Sat now and we've handed in all our surplus kit and are quite ready). I'll write them at home to send you a copy of my poems, one called 'Spring 1916' [see p. 86] I particularly like, and I think you will. But some poems will be in cloth and I am charging for those to make up the cost of printing. If you want any will you write me when I let you know where I am. They are 4/6 each. The king inspected us Thursday. I believe it[']s the first Bantam Brigade been inspected. He must have waited for us to stand up a good while. At a distance we look like soldiers sitting down, you know, legs so short.

Yours sincerely

Isaac Rosenberg

[*Postmarked June 15, 1916*]   22311 Pte I Rosenberg
                                                     A. Coy 11th(S) Batt. K.O.R.L
                                                     British Expeditionary Force

DEAR MR TREVELYAN

My sister sent me on your letter, which has made me feel very conceited and elated. It is strange why people should be so timid and afraid to praise on their own, and yet so bold to criticise. I know my faults are legion; a good many must be put down to the rotten conditions I wrote it in – the whole thing was written in barracks, and I suppose you know what an ordinary soldier's life is like. Moses symbolises the fierce desire for virility, and original action in contrast to slavery of the most abject kind. I was very sorry to hear about Bottomley being bad. I hope by the time this reaches you that will be a thing to joke about. If I get through this affair without any broken bones etc, I have a lot to say and one or two shilling shockers, that'll make some people jump. Here's a sketch of our passage over ['The Troop Ship', see p. 83]. If you see Mrs Rodker please ask her to write to me about R. as I believe R is in prison.

The above address will or should find me.

Yours sincerely

ISAAC ROSENBERG

We are in the trenches now and it[']s raining horribly.

To Miss Seaton [*from France, June 1916*]

We made straight for the trenches, but we've had vile weather, and I've been wet through for four days and nights. I lost all my socks and things before I left England, and hadn't the chance to make it up again, so I've been in trouble, particularly with bad heels; you can't have the slightest conception of what such an apparently trivial thing means. We've had shells bursting two yards off, bullets whizzing all over the show, but all you are aware of is the agony of your heels . . . I had a letter from R. C. Trevelyan, the poet . . . He writes: 'It is a long time since I have read anything that has impressed me so much as your "Moses" and some of your short poems . . .' He confesses parts are difficult, and he is not sure whether it's my fault or his.

[*No date*]   22311 A Coy 3 platoon
                                           11th K.O.R.L. B.E.F.

Dear Mrs Cohen

We are on a long march and I'm writing this on the chance of getting it off; so you should know I received your papers and also your letter. The notice in the Times of your book is true – especially about your handling of metre. It is an interesting number. The Poetry Review you sent is good – the articles are too breathless, and want more packing, I think. The poems by the soldier are vigorous but, I feel a bit commonplace. I did not like Rupert Brooke's beglo-ried sonnets for the same reason. What I mean is second hand phrases 'lambent fires' etc takes from its reality and strength. It should be approached in a colder way, more abstract, with less of the million feelings everybody feels; or all these should be concentrated in one distinguished emotion. Walt Whitman in 'Beat, drums, beat', has said the noblest thing on war.

I am glad Yeats liked your play: His criticism is an honour. He is the established great man and it is a high thing to receive praise from him. Don't talk of [Alfred] Noyes – he only cloys. I always think of some twopenny bazaar when I read him.

I am thinking of a Jewish play with Judas Macabeas [*sic*] for hero. I can put a lot in I've learnt out here. I hope I get the chance to go on with it. I've freshly written this thing – red from the anvil ['August 1914', see p. 84]. I have a good one in the anvil now but it wants knocking into shape. Thanks very much for the papers[.]

                    Yours sincerely

                                           Isaac Rosenberg

To Gordon Bottomley [postmarked July 23, 1916]

Your letter came to-day with Mr. Trevelyan's, like two friends to take me for a picnic. Or rather like friends come to release the convict from his chains with his innocence in their hands, as one sees in the twopenny picture palace. You might say, friends come to take you to church, or the priest to the prisoner. Simple *poetry* – that is where an interesting complexity of thought is kept in tone and right value to the dominating idea so that it is understandable and still ungraspable. I know it is beyond my reach just now, except, perhaps, in bits. I am always afraid of being empty. When I get more leisure in more settled times I will work on a larger scale and give myself room; then I may be less frustrated in my efforts to be clear, and satisfy myself too. I think what you say about getting beauty by phrasing of passages rather than the placing of individual words very fine and very true.

Aug 4th [*1916*]   [*Address in final paragraph*]

MY DEAR MARSH

I have only just received your letter, which has been lying about for the last week before it was given to me. By now, you must have read a letter I wrote on behalf of a friend, and sent to Whitehall to reach you during the day, as it was so pressing. I trust you have been able to do something; as it is rough luck on the poor fellow. I was most glad to get your letter and criticism. You know the conditions I have always worked under, and particularly with this last lot of poems. You know how earnestly one must wait on ideas, (you cannot coax real ones to you) and let as it were, a skin grow naturally round and through them. If you are not free, you can only, when the ideas come hot, seize them with the skin in tatters raw, crude, in some parts beautiful in others monstrous. Why print it then? Because those rare parts must not be lost. I work more and more as I write into more depth and lucidity, I am sure. I have a fine idea for a most gorgeous play, Adam and Lilith. If I could get a few months after the war to work and absorb myself completely into the thing, I'd write a great thing.

I am enclosing a poem ['Break of Day in the Trenches', see p. 90] I wrote in the trenches, which is surely as simple as ordinary talk. You might object to the second line as vague, but that was the best way I could express the sense of dawn.

Since I wrote last I have been given a job behind the lines and very rarely go into the trenches. My address is c/o 40th Divisional Coy Officer. B.E.F. Pte I Rosenberg 22311. It is more healthy but not absolutely safe from shells as we get those noisy visitors a good many times a day even here.

Yours sincerely

ISAAC ROSENBERG

[August 1916] [No address]

DEAR MR SCHIFF

Many thanks for your letter and the papers. I'll wait till I get back to England to learn French as I can't concentrate on it here. The French poets I think have given a nasty turn to English thought. It is all Café Royal poetry now. The Germans are far finer though they are fine through Baudelaire. Heine, our own Heine, we must say nothing of. I admire him more for always being a Jew at heart than anything else. Personally I am very fond of our Celtic Rabelais. Of Butler I know very little, but Shaw in spite of his topsy turvy manner seems to me to be very necessary. Anyhow his plays are the only plays I can stand at the theatre. I mean of course of the plays that are played on the stage. He has no subtlety, no delicate irony, none of the rarer qualities. But his broad satire is good.

Yours sincerely,

I. ROSENBERG

[August 1916] 22311

A Coy 3 Platoon
11th K.O.R.L. B.E.F.

MY DEAR MARSH

I know the terrible length of my new address will make an excellent excuse for not replying; I hope however, it will not frighten you. I am back again in the trenches. I have a notion the Artist rifles have been somewhere about because I fancy I recognized a Fitzroy Street flea, but I couldn't swear to it. I have been forbidden to send poems home, as the censor won't be bothered with going through such rubbish, or I would have sent you one I wrote about our armies, which I am rather bucked about. I have asked the 'Nation' to print it, if they do, you will see it there. The 'Georgian book' was sent out to me here. Brooke's poem on 'Clouds' is magnificent. Gordon Bottomley has been writing me warm letters. He is a great man and I feel most pained about his condition. Do you know anything about artists out here to disguise things, landscape sheds etc. Col S J Solomon is their Chief I believe and I know him a bit. I wonder if I'd be any good at it. Who would I have to approach about it. Do write.

Yours sincerely

ISAAC ROSENBERG

[*No date*]

22311. A Coy. 11th Batt. K.O.R.L. rgt
3 Platoon
British Expeditionary Force
France

DEAR MR TREVELYAN

My sister sent me your letter on, which I answered; but as certain other letters I sent off at the same time went astray I surmise that one was lost as well, so I am writing again. The other side of this sheet is a very crude sketch of how I look here in this dugout. I'll write out at the end of this letter a little poem ['The Troop Ship', see p. 83] of the troop ship where I try to describe in words the contortions we get into to try and wriggle ourselves into a little sleep. Of course if you're lucky and get a decent dugout you sleep quite easily – when you get the chance, otherwise you must sleep standing up, or sitting down, which latter is my case now. I must say that it has made me very happy to know you like my work so much; very few people do, or, at least, say so; and I believe I am a poet.

Here in the trenches where we are playing this extraordinary gamble, your letter made me feel refreshed and fine. I hope Bottomley is quite better by now – he is a man whose work (I have only read 'Chambers of Imagery') has made me feel more rare and delicately excited feelings, than any poetry I have ever read. The little poem 'Nimrod' the image in the first stanza to me is one of the most astonishing in all literature. Another thing that seems to me too astounding for comment, is Abercrombie's Hymn to Love.

I hope we may some day be able to talk these things over.

Yours sincerely

ISAAC ROSENBERG

Letter to R. C. Trevelyan, no date but late 1916, with pencil sketch of himself in dug-out (Imperial War Museum).

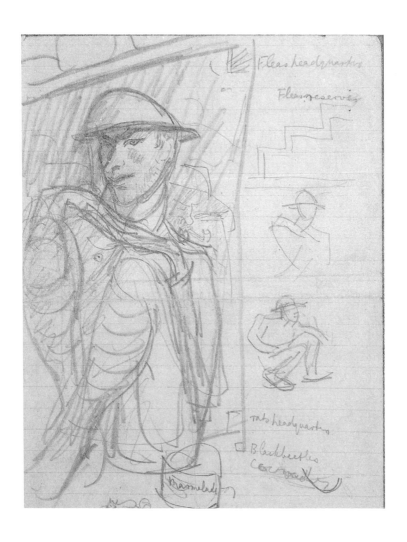

[*No date*]   22311 A Coy. 3. Platoon
                                    11th. Batt. K.O.R.L.
                                            B.E.F.

DEAR SONIA

I have been anxious to hear from you about Rodker. I wrote to Trevelyan (he thinks me a big knut at poetry) and asked him for news but I fancy my letter got lost. Write me any news – anything. I seem to have been in France, ages. I wish Rodker were with me, the infernal lingo is a tragedy with me and he'd help me out. If I was taciturn in England I am 10 times so here; our struggle to express ourselves is a fearful joke. However our wants are simple, our cash is scarce, and our time is precious, so French would perhaps be superfluous. I'd hardly believe French manners are so different to ours, but I leave all this for conversation. Here's a little poem a bit commonplace I'm afraid ['In the Trenches', see p. 89].

Yours sincerely

ISAAC ROSENBERG

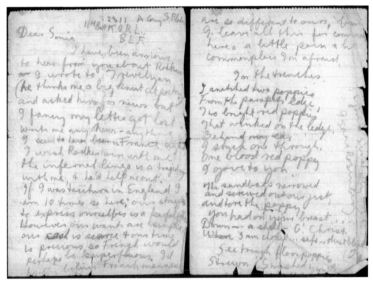

Letter to Sonia Rodker, no date but late 1916 (Imperial War Museum).

To Laurence Binyon [Autumn 1916]

It is far, very far, to the British Museum from here (situated as I am, Siberia is no further and certainly no colder), but not too far for that tiny mite of myself, my letter, to reach there. Winter has found its way into the trenches at last, but I will assure you, and leave to your imagination, the transport of delight with which we welcomed its coming. Winter is not the least of the horrors of war. I am determined that this war, with all its powers for devastation, shall not master my poeting; that is, if I am lucky enough to come through all right. I will not leave a corner of my consciousness covered up, but saturate myself with the strange and extraordinary new conditions of this life, and it will all refine itself into poetry later on. I have thoughts of a play round our Jewish hero, Judas Maccabeus. I have much real material here, and also there is some parallel in the savagery of the invaders then to this war. I am not decided whether truth of period is a good quality or a negative one. Flaubert's 'Salambo' [*sic*] proves, perhaps, that it is good. It decides the tone of the work, though it makes it hard to give the human side and make it more living. However, it is impossible now to work and difficult even to think of poetry, one is so cramped intellectually.

[*No date*]   Pte I Rosenberg
                                   [Address deleted by the censor.]

DEAR MR TREVELYAN

Your letter came with a second one of Bottomley's. His first was all praise and his second all criticism; but his criticism was higher praise than any praise I had been given before. His letter was full of fine writing and useful tips and I feel very grateful for it, and to you for first showing my things to him. I had been meaning to write to him for some time, in fact, when I first read him, but I always thought to myself, – wait till you have something worthy to show him! It was only coming out to France and the risk of being knocked over made me print the poems hurriedly.

I have never read B's plays though Mr Marsh told me of them, but the war interfered and I have read no literature for the last year, till I got

161

yours and B's letters. I have asked my sister to send you a poem Bottomley liked – 'Break of day in the trenches' [see page 90][.] Perhaps the end is not quite clear and wants working on. I have an idea for a book of war poems. I have already written a few small things but have plans for a few longish dramatic poems. Abercrombie's 'Hymn to Love' is I think, the great thing of modern times, and far above anything else of his I know. Bottomley is more profound and a purer artist – but the Hymn to Love wants some licking. Thank you for showing my work about, I am naturally anxious for discerning people to read my things.

Yours sincerely

ISAAC ROSENBERG

I have not heard from J.R. [John Rodker] and am glad he is not in trouble.

[Postmarked January 18, 1917]   *[Address given below]*

MY DEAR MARSH

My sister wrote me she would be writing to you. She'd got the idea of my being in vile health from your letter addressed to Dempsey St, and naturally they at home exaggerated things in their minds. Perhaps though it is not so exaggerated. That my health is undermined I feel sure of; but I have only lately been medically examined, and absolute fitness was the verdict. My being trans-fer[r]ed may be the consequence of my reporting sick, or not; I don't know for certain. But though this work does not entail half the hard-ships of the trenches, the winter and the conditions naturally tells on me, having once suffered from weak lungs, as you know. I have been in the trenches most of the 8 months I've been here, and the continual damp and exposure is whispering to my old friend con-sumption, and he may hear the words they say in time. I have nothing outwardly to show yet, but I feel it inwardly. I don't know what you could do in a case like this; perhaps I could be made use of as a draughtsman at home; or something else in my own line, or perhaps on munitions. My new address is

Pte I R 22311
7 Platoon F. Coy
40th Division

Works Battalion

B.E.F.

I wrote a poem some while ago which Bottomley liked so, and I want you to see it, but I'm writing in most awkward conditions and can't copy it now. 'Poetry' of Chicago printed a couple of my things ['Marching' and 'Break of Day in the Trenches', see pp. 78 and 90] and are paying me. I should think you find the Colonial Office interesting particularly after the war.

I hope however it leaves you leisure for literature; for me it[']s the great thing.

Yours sincerely

ISAAC ROSENBERG

To Gordon Bottomley [*postmarked April 8, 1917*]

All through this winter I have felt most crotchety, all kinds of small things interfering with my fitness. My hands would get chilblains or bad boots would make my feet sore; and this aggravating a general run down-ness, I have not felt too happy. I have gone less warmly clad during the winter than through the summer, because of the increased liveliness on my clothes. I've been stung to what we call 'dumping' a great part of my clothing, as I thought it wisest to go cold than lousy. It may have been this that caused all the crotchetiness. However, we've been in no danger – that is, from shell-fire – for a good long while, though so very close to most terrible fighting. But as far as houses or sign of ordinary human living is concerned, we might as well be in the Sahara Desert. I think I could give some blood-curdling touches if I wished to tell all I see, of dead buried men blown out of their graves, and more, but I will spare you all this.

[*Postmarked April 25, 1917*]   [*Address given below*]

MY DEAR MARSH

My sister wrote me you have been getting more of my 'Moses'. It is hardy of you, indeed, to spread it about; and I certainly would be distressed if I were the cause of a war in England; seeing what warfare means here. But it greatly pleases me, none the less, that this child of my brain should be seen and perhaps his beauties be discovered. His creator is in sadder plight; the harsh and unlovely times have made his mistress, the flighty Muse, abscond and elope with luckier rivals, but surely I shall hunt her and chase her somewhere into the summer and sweeter times. Anyway this is a strong hope; Lately I have not been very happy, being in torture with my feet again. The coldness of the weather and the weight of my boots have put my feet in a rotten state. My address is different now

Pte IR 22311

7 Platoon

120th Brigade Works Coy

B.E.F.

There is more excitement now, but though I enjoy this, my feet cause me great suffering and my strength is hardly equal to what is required.

I hear pretty often from G. Bottomley and his letters are like a handshake: and passages are splendid pieces of writing. Have you seen Trevelyan's 'Annual' which G.B. writes me of?

Do write me when you can.

Yours sincerely

Isaac Rosenberg

[*Postmarked May 8, 1917*]   [*No address*]

My Dear Marsh

We are camping in the woods now and are living great. My feet are almost healed now and my list of complaints has dwindled down to almost invisibility. I've written some lines suggested by going out wiring, or rather carrying wire up the line on limbers and running over dead bodies lying about [see 'Dead Man's Dump', p. 101]. I don't think what I've written is very good but I think the substance is, and when I work on it I'll make it fine. Bottomley told me he had some very old poems in The Annual but of course it[']s too bulky to send out here. Your extract from his 'Atlantis' is real Bottomleyian. The young Oxford poets you showed my things to I've never come across yet, and I'll soon begin to think myself a poet if my things get admired so.

I'm writing to my sister to send you the lines as she will type several copies.

Yours sincerely

I R

I trust the colonial office agrees with you

[*Postmarked May 27, 1917*] [*No address*]

MY DEAR MARSH

I liked your criticism of 'Dead mans dump'. Mr Binyon has often sermonised lengthily over my working on two different principles in the same thing and I know how it spoils the unity of a poem. But if I couldn't before, I can now, I am sure, plead the absolute necessity of fixing an idea before it is lost, because of the situation it[']s conceived in. Regular rhythms I do not like much, but of course it depends on where the stress and accent are laid. I think there is nothing finer than the vigorous opening of Lycidas for music; yet it is regular. Now I think if Andrew Marvell had broken up his rhythms more he would have been considered a terrific poet. As it is I like his poem urging his mistress to love because they have not a thousand years to love on and he can't afford to wait. (I forget the name of the poem ['To His Coy Mistress'] well I like it more than Lycidas.

I have written a much finer poem ['Daughters of War', see p. 107] which I've asked my sister to send you. Don't think from this I've time to write. This last poem is only about 70 lines and I started it about October. It is only when we get a bit of rest and the others might be gambling or squabbling I add a line or two, and continue this way. The weather is gorgeous now and we are bivouacked in the fields. The other night I awoke to find myself floating about with the water half over me. I took my shirt off and curled myself up on a little mound that the water hadn't touched and slept stark naked that night. But that was not all of the fun. The chap next to me was suddenly taken with Diarrhoea and kept on lifting the sheet of the Bivouac, and as I lay at the end the rain came beating on my nakedness all night. Next morning, I noticed the poor chap's discoloured pants hanging on a bough near by, and I thought after all I had the best of it.

I fancy you will like my last poem, I am sure it is at least as good as my Kolue speech [from *Moses*], and there is more of it.

Yours sincerely

ISAAC ROSENBERG

To Gordon Bottomley [?July–August 1917]

The other poems I have not yet read, but I will follow on with letters and shall send the bits of – or rather the bit of – a play I've written. Just now it is interfered with by a punishment I am under-going for the offence of being endowed with a poor memory, which continually causes me trouble and often punishment. I forgot to wear my gas-helmet one day; in fact, I've often forgotten it, but I was noticed one day, and seven days' pack drill is the consequence, which I do between the hours of going up the line and sleep. My memory, always weak, has become worse since I've been out here.

[*1917, ?July*]

22311 Pte I Rosenberg
11th K.O.R.L. Regt.
Attached 229 Field Coy, R.Es.
B.E.F. France

DEAR MR SCHIFF

I was most glad to hear from you. I have just received your letter and its useful enclosure for which many thanks. I say I was most glad – but that is not quite true – your letter is too bitter. I did not get your letters in France and I often wondered about you, but things are so tumultuous and disturbing that unless one has everything handy, like an addressed envelope a pencil and a moment to spare one cannot write letters. One's envelopes get stuck and useless with the damp and you cannot replace them. I managed to jot down some ideas for poems now and then but I won[']t send them to you because they are actual transcripts of the battlefield and you won[']t like that, anyway just now. I do hope you have exaggerated your feel-ings and are not so low in spirits as your letter makes out. We manage to keep cheerful out here in the face of most horrible things but then,

Pencil self-portrait in cap, profile, inscribed in Rosenberg's hand
'I. R. France July 1917' (Imperial War Museum).

we are kept busy, and have no time to brood. I hope your wife is well. My sister and my mother wish you well.

Yours sincerely

ISAAC ROSENBERG

I am sending you a good photo of myself in a day or two.

[*Postmarked July 30, 1917*]   [*Address given below*]

MY DEAR MARSH

I'm glad you've got your old job again and are Winston Churchill's private sec. once more, though it will be a pity if it will interfere with your literary projects. I thought that would happen when I heard he'd become Minister of Munitions. I can imagine how busy you will be kept and if you still mean to go on with your memoir and G.P. [*Georgian Poetry*]; you perhaps can imagine me, though of course my work pretty much leaves my brain alone especially as I have a decent job now and am not as rushed and worked as I was in the trenches. I will be glad to be included in the Georgian Book, and hope your other work won't interfere with it. I've asked my sister (she recognises your helplessness about me, but I hope you were not too annoyed at her persistence; although I was; when I heard of it) not to send the Amulet because I've changed the idea completely and I think if I can work it out on the new lines it will be most clear and most extraordinary. It[']s called 'The Unicorn' now. I am stuck in the most difficult part; I have to feel a set of unusual emotions which I simply can't feel yet. However if I keep on thinking about it it may come. We may not begin a letter with our address but work it in the text; I generally forget about it as I go on writing.

Pte I.R. 22311
11th K.O.R.L.
Attached 229 Field Coy R.E.s.
B.E.F.

I think with you that poetry should be definite thought and clear expression, however subtle; I don't think there should be any vagueness at all; but a sense of something hidden and felt to be there; Now when my things fail to be clear I am sure it is because of the luckless choice of a word or the failure to introduce a word that would flash my idea plain, as it is to my own mind. I believe my Amazon poem ['Daughters of War', see p. 107] to be my best poem. If there is any difficulty it must be in words here and there[,] the changing or elimination of which may make the poem clear. It has taken me about a year to write; for I have changed and rechanged it and thought hard over that poem and striven to get that sense of inexorableness the human (or inhuman) side of this war has. It even penetrates behind human life for the 'Amazon' who speaks in the second part of the poem is imagined to be without her lover yet, while all her sisters have theirs, the released spirits of the slain earth men; her lover yet remains to be released. I hope however to be home on leave, and talk it over, some time this side of the year. In my next letter I will try and send an idea of 'The Unicorn'.

If you are too busy don't bother about answering;

Yours sincerely

Isaac Rosenberg

[*Received August 11, 1917*]   [*No address*]

Dear Father

Ray [his sister Rachel] wrote me card of the air raid, also your letter. Your miracle amused me very much and the story of the honey delighted me. I hope to be home before the new year but leaves are going very slowly in our division. So it[']s no use building on it. Mrs. Herbert Cohen sent me a little book compiled by the Chief Rabbi of Jewish interest. There are good bits from the Talmud and from some old writers. A very little bit by Heine, nothing by Disraeli and a lot by Mr. Hertz and a few more rash people; I admire their daring, if not their judgement. Mrs. Cohen has paid all the expenses and a fuller anthology is coming out shortly; I hope some restraint and caution will be used this time. I think you will find Heine's poems among my books, there is a beautiful poem called 'Princess Sabbath' among them, where the Jew who is a dog all the week, Sabbath night when the candles are lit, is transformed into a gorgeous prince to meet his bride the Sabbath.

I mention this because there is a feeble imitation of this in the

169

anthology. If I am lucky and get home this side of the year you might keep Dave's breeches for me.

Love to all

ISAAC

To Gordon Bottomley [on leave, September 21, 1917]

The greatest thing of my leave after seeing my mother was your letter which has just arrived . . . I wish I could have seen you, but now I must go on and hope that things will turn out well, and some happy day will give me the chance of meeting you . . . I am afraid I can do no writing or reading; I feel so restless here and un-anchored. We have lived in such an elemental way so long, things here don't look quite right to me somehow; or it may be the consciousness of my so limited time here for freedom – so little time to do so many things bewilders me. 'The Unicorn', as will be obvious, is just a basis; its final form will be very different, I hope.

[1917, ? November]   *[Address as given below]*

DEAR MOTHER

Rec Parcel – everything in it champion – but really there is no need to send butter, eggs or Borsht, just now, at any rate. I suppose we get our food much easier than you – and in this village we get any amount of extra. I have not heard from Samuels so don't know whether he is Colonel of the Batt. I applied for a transfer about a month ago but I fancy it fell through. I shall apply again. Neither Mrs. Cohen or Löwy have written to me though I have written. You can let them have my new address if you care to. Did you come across any notices of my thing in the Georgian Book? I don't know who the Sergeant was Annie saw – several are on leave now – they mostly live in the North of England though. I hope our Russian cousins are happy now. Trotsky, I imagine will look after the interests of his co religionists – Russia is like an amputated limb to our cause and America is the cork substitute: I doubt whether she is more. 8 Platoon B Coy 1st Batt. K.O.R.L. B.E.F.[.] I hope you

Rosenberg in uniform of the K.O.R.L., with cap, inscribed in his hand 'To Gordon Bottomley from Isaac Rosenberg, Sept. 1917' (Imperial War Museum).

manage to get things all right and comfortably. We hear such rotten tales about home. Love to all

Isaac

To Miss Seaton [*written in Hospital, Autumn 1917*]

I was very glad to have your letter and know there is no longer a mix-up about letters and suchlike. Always the best thing to do is to answer at once, that is the likeliest way of catching one, for we shift about so quickly; how long I will stay here I cannot say: it may be a while or just a bit. I have some Shakespeare: the Comedies and also 'Macbeth'. Now I see your argument and cannot deny my treatment of your criticisms, but have you ever asked yourself why I always am rude to your criticisms? Now, I intended to show you —'s letters [Bottomley's or Trevelyan's] and why I value his criticisms. I think anybody can pick holes and find unsound parts in any work of art; anyone can say Christ's creed is a slave's creed, the Mosaic is a vindictive, savage creed, and so on. It is the unique and superior, the illuminating qualities one wants to find – discover the direction of the impulse. Whatever anybody thinks of a poet he will always know himself: he knows that the most marvellously expressed idea is still nothing; and it is stupid to think that praise can do him harm. I know sometimes one cannot exactly define one's feelings nor explain reasons for liking and disliking; but there is then the right of a suspicion that the thing has not been properly understood or one is prejudiced. It is much my fault if I am not understood, I know; but I also feel a kind of injustice if my idea is not grasped and is ignored, and only petty cavilling at form, which I had known all along was so, is continually knocked into me. I feel quite sure that form is only a question of time. I am afraid I am more rude than ever, but I have exaggerated here the difference between your criticisms and —'s. Ideas of poetry can be very different too. Tennyson thought Burns' love-songs important, but the 'Cottar's S.N.' poor. Wordsworth thought the opposite.

172

To Miss Seaton [written in Hospital, November 15, 1917]

London may not be the place for poetry to keep healthy in, but Shakespeare did most of his work there, and Donne, Keats, Milton, Blake – I think nearly all our big poets. But, after all, that is a matter of personal likings or otherwise. Most of the French country I have seen has been devastated by war, torn up – even the woods look ghastly with their shell-shattered trees; our only recollections of warm and comfortable feelings are the rare times amongst human villages, which happened about twice in a year; but who can tell what one will like or do after the war? If the twentieth century is so awful, tell me what period you believe most enviable. Even Pater points out the Renaissance was not an outburst – it was no simultaneous marked impulse of minds living in a certain period of time – but scattered and isolated.

To Miss Seaton [November–December 1917]

Many thanks for book and chocolate. Both are being devoured with equal pleasure. I can't get quite the delight in Whitman as from one poem of his I know – 'Captain my Captain'. I admire the vigour and independence of his mind, but his diction is so diffused. Emerson and not Whitman is America's poet. You will persist in refusing to see my side of our little debate on criticism. Everybody has agreed with you about the faults, and the reason is obvious; the faults are so glaring that nobody can fail to see them. But how many have seen the beauties? And it is here more than the other that the true critic shows himself. And I absolutely disagree that it is blindness or carelessness; it is the brain succumbing to the herculean attempt to enrich the world of ideas.

To Miss Seaton [dated February 14, 1918]

We had a rough time in the trenches with the mud, but now we're out for a bit of a rest, and I will try and write longer letters. You must know by now what a rest behind the line means. I can call the evenings – that is, from tea to lights out – my own; but there is no chance whatever for seclusion or any hope of writing poetry now. Sometimes I give way and am appalled at the devastation this life seems to have made in my nature. It seems to have blunted me. I seem to be powerless to compel my will to any direction, and all I do is without energy and interest.

[*Early March, 1918*]   [*Address as below*]

Dear Rodker

I could not answer your last letter as immediately as I wished because of a lot of unexpected things. Things happen so suddenly here that really nothing is unexpected – but what I mean is quite a lot of changes came on top of each other and interfered with my good epistolary intentions. I hope you still keep the same good spirits of your last letter and that the work is not beyond your strength. My work is but somehow we blunder through. From hospital I went back to the line and we had a rough time with the mud. Balzac could give you the huge and terrible sensations of sinking in the mud. I was in the trenches a month when our Batt broke up and I am now in another Batt of our regiment. When you write again write to

Pte I Rosenberg 22311
8 Platoon. B. Coy
1st Batt K.O.R.L.
B.E.F.

Just now we're out for a rest and I hope the warmer weather sets in when we go up the line again. It is quite impossible to write or think of writing stuff now, so I can only hope for hospital or the end of the war if I want to write. In hospital I saw the Georgian Book. Turner is pretty good – but somehow I seem to have lost all sense of discrimination and everything seems good. My own is so fragmentary that I think it were better left out. I hear it is selling well. You have got an article on Trevelyan, I hear. He sent me his Comedy which I liked very much. I know little of his other work.

Yours sincerely

Isaac Rosenberg

To Gordon Bottomley [*dated March 7, 1918*]

I believe our interlude is nearly over, and we may go up the line
any moment now, so I answer your letter straightaway. If only this
war were over our eyes would not be on death so much: it seems to
underlie even our underthoughts. Yet when I have been so near to
it as anybody could be, the idea has never crossed my mind, cer-
tainly not so much as when some lying doctor told me I had con-
sumption. I like to think of myself as a poet; so what you say, though
I know it to be extravagant, gives me immense pleasure.

To Miss Seaton [*March 8, 1918*]

I do not feel that I have much to say, but I do know that unless
I write now it will be a long time before you hear from me again,
without something exceptional happens. It is not very cold now, but
I dread the wet weather, which is keeping off while we are out, and,
I fear, saving itself up for us. We will become like mummies – look
warm and lifelike, but a touch and we crumble to pieces. Did I send
you a little poem, 'The Burning of the Temple' [see p. 111]? I
thought it was poor, or rather, difficult in expression, but G.
Bottomley thinks it fine. Was it clear to you? If I am lucky, and come
off undamaged, I mean to put all my innermost experiences into the
'Unicorn'. I want it to symbolize the war and all the devastating
forces let loose by an ambitious and unscrupulous will. Last summer
I wrote pieces for it and had the whole of it planned out, but since
then I've had no chance of working on it and it may have gone quite
out of my mind.

[*Postmarked March 7, 1918*]   [*Address given below*]

MY DEAR MARSH

I see my sister has been on the warpath again, and after your
scalp in her sisterly regard for me. They know my lackadaisical ways
at home and have their own methods of forcing me to act. I have now
put in for a transfer to the Jewish Batt – which I think is in

Mesopotamia now. I think I should be climatized to the heat after my S. African experience. I'll let you know if I get it. I am now in

8 Platoon, B Coy

1st. K.O.R.L. B.E.F.

as our old Batt broke up.

I saw the G.B. [the third volume of *Georgian Poetry*]. It does not match the first G.B. nor indeed any of the others in my mind. But I put that down to the War of course. Turner is very poetic. Masefield sentimentalizes in too Elizabethan a fashion. There is a vivid poem about Christ in the Tower [by Robert Nichols] I remember I liked very much. And of course G.B.'s [Gordon Bottomley's] 'Atlantis' stands out. I saw the book about 3 months ago and not for long. I was going into the trenches then. What have you done with your 'Life of R.B.' [Rupert Brooke] is it complete yet[?]

I'm sending this letter to Ministry of Mun. because I sent a letter a month or so ago to Raymond Buildings and got no answer. If you are very busy do try and drop just a line so that I know you've rec my letter.

Yours sincerely

I ROSENBERG

[*Postmarked April 2, 1918*]   *28th March*

MY DEAR MARSH

I think I wrote you I was about to go up the line again after our little rest. We are now in the trenches again and though I feel very sleepy, I just have a chance to answer your letter so I will while I may. It[']s really my being lucky enough to bag an inch of candle that incites me to this pitch of punctual epistolary [*sic*]. I must measure my letter by the light. First, this is my address

22311 Pte I R.

6 Platoon B Coy 1st K.O.R.L.

B.E.F.

We are very busy just now and poetry is right out of our scheme. I wrote one or two things in hospital about Xmas time but I don't remember whether I sent them to you or not. I'll send one, anyhow.

During our little interlude of rest from the line I managed to do a bit of sketching – somebody had colours – and they weren't so bad, I don't think I have forgotten my art after all. I've heard nothing further about the J.B. [The Jewish Battalion] and of course feel annoyed – more because no reasons have been given me – but when we leave the trenches, I'll enquire further. I don't remember reading [John] Freeman. I wanted to write a battle song for the Judaens [*sic*] but can think of nothing strong and wonderful enough yet. Here's just a slight thing ['Through these pale cold days', see p. 113, the last poem Rosenberg wrote; he was killed in action the day before this letter was posted].

I've seen no poetry for ages now so you mustn't be too critical – My vocabulary small enough before is impoverished and bare.

Yours sincerely

I ROSENBERG

Isaac Rosenberg (seated) with his brother David.

INDEX OF FIRST LINES